# Botswana and Travel Guide 2025

A No-Nonsense Handbook: Must-See Attractions, Packing Essential, Hidden Gems, Affordable Stays, Culture-Filled Adventures and Botswana & Namibia's Best-Kept Secrets

# Damien Gomez

## Copyright Notice

No part of this book may be reproduced, written, electronic, recorded, or photocopied without written permission from the publisher or author.

The exception would be in the case of brief quotations embodied in critical articles or reviews and pages where permission is specifically granted by the publisher or author.

Although every precaution has been taken to verify the accuracy of the information contained herein, the author and publisher assume no responsibility for any errors or omissions. No liability is assumed for damages that may result from the use of the information contained within.

All Rights Reserved ©2025 Damien Gomez

# TABLE OF CONTENT

| | |
|---|---|
| **INTRODUCTION** | **11** |
| About This Guide | 12 |
| Why Visit Botswana & Namibia? | 13 |
| Best Time to Visit | 14 |
| Travel Essentials & Packing List | 16 |
| **CHAPTER 1: PLANNING YOUR TRIP** | **19** |
| Visa Requirements & Entry Regulations | 19 |
| Health & Safety Precautions | 21 |
| Budgeting & Cost Estimates for Botswana & Namibia | 23 |
| Best Travel Insurance Options | 25 |
| Transportation: Flights, Buses, and Car Rentals | 26 |
| **CHAPTER 2: GETTING AROUND** | **29** |
| Domestic Flights & Regional Airlines | 29 |
| Public Transport: Buses & Shared Taxis | 30 |
| Self-Driving Tips & Road Conditions | 31 |
| Border Crossings & Customs Regulations | 32 |
| Travel Apps & Navigation Tools | 34 |
| **CHAPTER 3: WHERE TO STAY** | **37** |
| Luxury Lodges & Resorts | 37 |
| Mid-Range Hotels & Guesthouses | 46 |
| Budget-Friendly Hostels & Campsites | 55 |
| Unique Stays: Safari Camps & Desert Lodges | 64 |
| Booking Tips & Recommendations | 71 |

## CHAPTER 4: TOP ATTRACTIONS IN BOTSWANA — 75

- CHOBE NATIONAL PARK & WILDLIFE SAFARI — 75
- OKAVANGO DELTA: MOKORO RIDES & GAME VIEWING — 77
- MOREMI GAME RESERVE & SAVUTI WILDLIFE — 80
- MAKGADIKGADI PANS & KUBU ISLAND — 82
- CENTRAL KALAHARI GAME RESERVE & DECEPTION VALLEY — 84

## CHAPTER 5: TOP ATTRACTIONS IN NAMIBIA — 87

- ETOSHA NATIONAL PARK & THE BIG FIVE — 87
- SOSSUSVLEI & DEADVLEI: NAMIBIA'S ICONIC DUNES — 89
- SKELETON COAST & SHIPWRECK ADVENTURES — 92
- FISH RIVER CANYON: AFRICA'S GRAND CANYON — 94
- DAMARALAND & TWYFELFONTEIN ROCK ENGRAVINGS — 97

## CHAPTER 6: OUTDOOR ACTIVITIES & ADVENTURE — 99

- SAFARI EXPERIENCES: GAME DRIVES & WALKING SAFARIS — 99
- HOT AIR BALLOON RIDES OVER THE DESERT: — 101
- QUAD BIKING IN THE NAMIB DESERT — 102
- CAMPING & OVERLANDING SAFARIS — 103
- KAYAKING & DOLPHIN WATCHING IN WALVIS BAY — 104
- HIKING TRAILS & MULTI-DAY TREKS — 105

## CHAPTER 7: CULTURE, HISTORY & LOCAL LIFE — 107

- INDIGENOUS TRIBES: SAN BUSHMEN, HIMBA & HERERO — 107
- TRADITIONAL MUSIC & DANCE — 109
- COLONIAL HISTORY & INDEPENDENCE MOVEMENTS — 110
- ART, HANDICRAFTS & LOCAL MARKETS — 112
- CULTURAL FESTIVALS & EVENTS — 113

## CHAPTER 8: FOOD & DINING EXPERIENCES — 117

| | |
|---|---|
| Traditional Dishes & Street Food | 117 |
| Fine Dining & Gourmet Safari Meals | 126 |
| Best Local Restaurants & Cafés | 127 |
| Wine & Beer Scene in Namibia & Botswana | 128 |
| Bush Cooking & Braai Culture | 130 |

## CHAPTER 9: SHOPPING & SOUVENIRS — 133

| | |
|---|---|
| Best Markets for Handcrafted Goods | 133 |
| Ethical Souvenir Shopping: What to Buy and What to Avoid | 135 |
| Famous Botswana & Namibian Gems & Jewelry | 136 |
| Leather, Textiles, and Wood Carvings | 137 |
| Where to Buy Local Art | 140 |

## CHAPTER 10: SUSTAINABLE & RESPONSIBLE TRAVEL — 143

| | |
|---|---|
| Eco-Lodges & Conservation Efforts | 143 |
| Ethical Wildlife Tourism | 144 |
| Supporting Local Communities | 147 |
| Minimizing Your Carbon Footprint | 149 |
| Volunteering & Giving Back | 150 |

## CHAPTER 11: 7-DAY COMBINED BOTSWANA & NAMIBIA ITINERARY 153

| | |
|---|---|
| Day 1: Arrival in Maun, Botswana & Okavango Delta Experience | 153 |
| Day 2: Mokoro Safari & Transfer to Moremi Game Reserve | 155 |
| Day 3: Moremi Game Reserve to Savuti, Chobe National Park | 157 |
| Day 4: Chobe River Safari & Transfer to Namibia (Caprivi Strip) | 158 |
| Day 5: Drive to Etosha National Park, Namibia | 160 |
| Day 6: Etosha Safari & Transfer to Swakopmund | 162 |
| Day 7: Sossusvlei Dunes & Departure from Windhoek | 164 |

## CHAPTER 12: TRAVEL TIPS & PRACTICAL INFORMATION — 167

| | |
|---|---|
| LANGUAGE & COMMUNICATION | 167 |
| CURRENCY & PAYMENT OPTIONS | 168 |
| ELECTRICITY & INTERNET CONNECTIVITY | 169 |
| TIPPING & LOCAL ETIQUETTE | 170 |
| EMERGENCY CONTACTS & USEFUL NUMBERS | 172 |

## CHAPTER 13: FREQUENTLY ASKED QUESTIONS (FAQS) — 175

| | |
|---|---|
| COMMON TRAVELER CONCERNS ANSWERED | 175 |
| SAFETY TIPS FOR SOLO TRAVELERS | 178 |
| FAMILY-FRIENDLY TRAVEL ADVICE | 180 |
| BEST TIMES TO VISIT SPECIFIC REGIONS | 182 |
| TRAVEL HACKS & MONEY-SAVING TIPS | 184 |

## CHAPTER 14: CONCLUSION — 187

| | |
|---|---|
| FINAL TRAVEL TIPS & RECOMMENDATIONS | 187 |
| REFLECTING ON YOUR BOTSWANA & NAMIBIA JOURNEY | 189 |
| ENCOURAGING SUSTAINABLE TRAVEL PRACTICES | 189 |
| HOW TO STAY CONNECTED WITH FELLOW TRAVELERS | 190 |
| RESOURCES FOR FURTHER EXPLORATION | 192 |

# INTRODUCTION

Are you tired of overpriced safari packages that don't deliver the authentic experience you crave? Do you struggle to find reliable information on the best-hidden gems in Botswana and Namibia? Worried about navigating border crossings and road conditions in remote areas? Unsure whether you should self-drive or join a guided tour? Do you want to witness Africa's most breathtaking landscapes without the tourist crowds? Frustrated by the lack of clear budgeting tips for both luxury and budget travelers? Concerned about safety, especially when exploring off-the-beaten-path destinations? Not sure what to pack for a trip that spans deserts, wetlands, and savannas? Curious about how to experience local cultures without feeling like a tourist?

If any of these questions sound familiar, you're in the right place. This no-nonsense travel guide to Botswana and Namibia is designed to cut through the clutter and give you the essential details you need. Whether you're a first-time visitor or a seasoned traveler, this book provides straightforward advice on must-see attractions, practical travel logistics, and hidden gems that most tourists overlook.

Botswana and Namibia offer some of the most awe-inspiring landscapes and wildlife experiences on the planet—from the lush Okavango Delta to the towering dunes of Sossusvlei. But exploring these destinations requires careful planning, especially when venturing into remote areas. That's where this guide comes in. You'll find expert tips on self-driving routes, affordable stays, cultural encounters, and adventure activities—all tailored to help you make the most of your trip.

No fluff, no filler—just the practical, reliable advice you need to experience Botswana and Namibia like a pro. Let's get started.

## About This Guide

This book is your ultimate travel companion for exploring Botswana and Namibia with confidence. Designed for both first-time visitors and seasoned adventurers, it cuts through the overwhelming amount of information out there and delivers clear, practical advice to help you plan an unforgettable trip.

Unlike generic travel guides, this no-nonsense handbook focuses on what truly matters:

**Must-see attractions** – From the Okavango Delta's winding waterways to Namibia's towering dunes, we highlight the best destinations worth your time and money.

**Hidden gems** – Discover lesser-known spots where you can escape the crowds and experience the raw beauty of Africa.

**Budget-friendly & luxury options** – Whether you're a backpacker or looking for five-star comfort, we provide accommodation recommendations for every budget.

**Practical travel tips** – Learn about visas, border crossings, self-driving routes, packing essentials, and local customs to ensure a smooth journey.

**Adventure & culture** – From thrilling safaris to meeting indigenous tribes, this guide helps you experience the best of both worlds.

Every section is designed to be **straightforward, engaging, and actionable**, so you can spend less time researching and more time experiencing the wild beauty of Botswana and Namibia. Whether you're planning a week-long safari or an extended overland adventure, this guide ensures you're well-prepared to make the most of your trip.

Now, let's start planning your adventure!

## Why Visit Botswana & Namibia?

Botswana and Namibia offer some of the most spectacular landscapes, diverse wildlife, and authentic cultural experiences in Africa. Whether you're an adventure seeker, a nature lover, or a cultural explorer, these two countries provide unforgettable experiences that few destinations can match.

### 1. World-Class Wildlife Safaris

Both countries are home to Africa's most iconic wildlife. Botswana's **Okavango Delta**, **Chobe National Park**, and **Moremi Game Reserve** offer some of the best game-viewing opportunities on the continent, with massive elephant herds, big cats, and rare wild dogs. Namibia's **Etosha National Park** is equally impressive, where animals gather around vast salt pans and floodlit waterholes, offering unique wildlife encounters.

### 2. Breathtaking Landscapes

From the towering **red dunes of Sossusvlei** to the eerie **Skeleton Coast**, Namibia boasts some of the most surreal and photogenic scenery in the world. Botswana, on the other hand, is home to **lush wetlands, vast salt pans, and arid deserts**, creating a stunning contrast of ecosystems within a single journey.

### 3. Off-the-Beaten-Path Adventure

If you crave adventure beyond typical safari experiences, Botswana and Namibia won't disappoint. **Self-driving through the Namib Desert, quad biking across the Makgadikgadi Pans, hot air ballooning over the Kalahari**, and **kayaking with seals in Walvis Bay** are just a few ways to explore these wild frontiers.

### 4. Rich Cultural Heritage

Both countries are home to fascinating indigenous communities. Visit the **San Bushmen of the Kalahari**, learn about the **Himba people's traditional way of life**, or explore the colonial influences in cities like Windhoek and Swakopmund.

### 5. Fewer Crowds, More Authenticity

Unlike other popular African safari destinations, Botswana and Namibia remain relatively untouched by mass tourism. You can enjoy vast, open landscapes and world-class wildlife encounters without the crowds.

### 6. Responsible & Sustainable Tourism

Botswana is a leader in **high-value, low-impact tourism**, ensuring that its pristine wilderness is protected while providing an exclusive experience. Namibia is the **first African country to integrate environmental conservation into its constitution**, making it a pioneer in community-based wildlife conservation.

### 7. Incredible Stargazing

With some of the darkest skies on Earth, Namibia's **NamibRand Nature Reserve** and Botswana's **Central Kalahari Game Reserve** offer unparalleled stargazing opportunities, where you can witness the Milky Way in breathtaking clarity.

## Best Time to Visit

The best time to visit Botswana and Namibia depends on what you want to experience—wildlife viewing, desert landscapes, or fewer crowds. Both countries have a **dry season (May–October)** and a **wet season (November–April),** each offering unique advantages.

### Best Overall Time: May – October (Dry Season)

**Why?** This is the peak season for safaris and outdoor adventures.

**What to Expect:** Clear skies, minimal rain, and excellent wildlife viewing as animals gather around water sources.

**Ideal for:** Safari lovers, self-drive travelers, and those looking for comfortable temperatures.

### Month-by-Month Breakdown

**May – June (Cool & Dry)**

Transition from wet to dry season; landscapes are still lush.

Fewer crowds, comfortable temperatures (10–25°C / 50–77°F).

Best for a mix of greenery and increasing wildlife sightings.

**July – September (Peak Safari Season)**

Prime wildlife viewing in **Chobe, Okavango Delta, and Etosha.**

Dry conditions make self-driving easier.

Cooler nights, pleasant days (15–30°C / 59–86°F).

Higher prices and more tourists—book early.

**October (Hot but Great Wildlife)**

Waterholes dry up, making wildlife spotting easy.

Rising temperatures (up to 35°C / 95°F), especially in Namibia.

Fewer tourists compared to July–September.

**November – April (Wet Season / Green Season)**

**Why Visit?** Lower prices, fewer crowds, and lush landscapes.

**What to Expect:** Afternoon showers, vibrant scenery, and the best birdwatching.

**Ideal for:** Budget travelers, photographers, and bird enthusiasts.

**November – December:** Start of rains; occasional storms but great wildlife sightings.

**January – March:** Peak of the rainy season; roads can be muddy, but fewer tourists.

**April:** Rains ease; landscapes remain green, and temperatures are moderate.

**Best Time for Specific Activities:**

**Safaris:** June – October

**Self-Driving:** May – September

**Birdwatching:** November – March

**Photography & Landscapes:** April – June (lush scenery, fewer tourists)

**Budget Travel:** November – April (lower prices on lodges and safaris)

# Travel Essentials & Packing List

**1. Travel Documents & Essentials**

Passport (valid for at least six months)

Visa (if required, check entry regulations)

Yellow Fever Certificate (if transiting from an endemic country)

Travel Insurance (covering medical emergencies, evacuation, and trip cancellations)

Driver's License & International Driving Permit (for self-driving trips)

Printed Copies of Travel Documents (passports, insurance, bookings)

Emergency Contacts & Itinerary Printout

**2. Clothing & Footwear**

**For Hot Days & Safaris (Light & Breathable)**

Lightweight, long-sleeved shirts (for sun and insect protection)

Breathable t-shirts (neutral colors to avoid attracting insects)

Convertible hiking pants & comfortable shorts

Wide-brim hat or cap

**For Cool Mornings & Evenings (Layering is Key)**

Fleece or lightweight jacket (it gets cold, especially in the desert)

Warm sweater for early game drives

Scarf, gloves & beanie (if visiting June–August)

**Footwear**

Sturdy hiking boots or trail shoes (for walking safaris & rough terrain)

Comfortable sandals or sneakers (for casual use)

**Additional Essentials**

Buff or bandana (for dust protection in desert areas)

Swimsuit (for lodges, pools, and coastal spots like Walvis Bay)

### 3. Health & First Aid

Prescription medications (bring extra supply)

Malaria prophylaxis (especially for Botswana)

High-SPF sunscreen & lip balm

Insect repellent (with DEET or Picaridin)

Basic first aid kit (bandages, antiseptic, pain relievers, diarrhea meds)

Electrolytes & rehydration salts (for hot weather)

Motion sickness pills (if doing boat safaris or bumpy drives)

### 4. Travel Gear & Accessories

Daypack or small backpack (for excursions)

Dry bag (for mokoro rides & boat trips)

Binoculars (for wildlife viewing)

Camera & extra memory cards (plus a dustproof bag for protection)

Headlamp or flashlight (with extra batteries)

Power bank & travel adapter (Type M / D for Botswana, Type D / M for Namibia)

Reusable water bottle (stay hydrated, reduce plastic use)

### 5. Money & Payments

Local currency (Botswana Pula & Namibian Dollar)

USD or Euros (widely accepted for major expenses)

Credit/debit cards (Visa & Mastercard preferred)

Small bills for tips, local markets, and rural areas

**6. Optional but Useful Items**

Travel laundry detergent & quick-dry towel

Guidebook or offline travel apps (like Maps.me)

Notebook & pen (for travel notes & journaling)

# Chapter 1: Planning Your Trip

## Visa Requirements & Entry Regulations

**1. Visa Requirements for Botswana**

**Visa-Free Entry:**

Citizens of **USA, UK, Canada, EU, Australia, New Zealand, South Africa**, and many other countries can enter Botswana **visa-free for up to 90 days** within a 12-month period.

Visitors must have a passport valid for at least **six months** beyond their date of entry and at least **two blank pages** for stamps.

**Visa on Arrival:**

Travelers who require a visa can apply for a **Visa on Arrival** at designated entry points. However, it's advisable to check in advance, as policies may change.

**eVisa & Pre-Arranged Visas:**

Some nationalities must apply for a visa **before arrival** through Botswana's online eVisa system or at an embassy.

Processing time varies but typically takes **7–14 working days**.

**Additional Entry Requirements:**

Proof of onward or return ticket

Hotel bookings or a letter of invitation from a host in Botswana

Sufficient funds to cover the stay

**Special Requirements for Minors:**

Children under **18 years** must present an **unabridged birth certificate** and, if traveling with one parent or a guardian, a **notarized consent letter** from the non-accompanying parent.

## 2. Visa Requirements for Namibia

**Visa-Free Entry:**

Citizens of **USA, UK, Canada, EU, Australia, New Zealand, South Africa**, and many other countries can enter **visa-free for up to 90 days** for tourism purposes.

A passport valid for **at least six months** and **two blank pages** is required.

**Visa on Arrival & Pre-Arranged Visas:**

Travelers from countries not eligible for visa-free entry must obtain a **Visa on Arrival** at international airports or apply for a **pre-arranged visa** through a Namibian embassy.

Visa processing time is usually **5–10 working days**.

**Additional Entry Requirements:**

Proof of onward or return travel

Sufficient funds for the duration of the stay

Address of accommodation in Namibia

**Special Requirements for Minors:**

Similar to Botswana, minors must present an **unabridged birth certificate** and parental consent documents if traveling with one parent or a guardian.

## 3. Entry Regulations & Border Control

**Yellow Fever Vaccination:** Required **only if** arriving from a country with risk of yellow fever transmission.

**Customs Regulations:** Duty-free limits apply for alcohol, tobacco, and certain goods. Importing fresh food items and animal products may be restricted.

**Border Crossings:**

Popular overland crossings include **Kazungula (Botswana–Namibia)** and **Ngoma Bridge (Botswana–Namibia)**.

Vehicle owners must carry **valid vehicle registration, insurance, and a cross-border permit** when self-driving.

### 4. Overstaying & Visa Extensions

Overstaying a visa can lead to **fines, deportation, or travel bans**.

Visa extensions for **Botswana** can be requested at the **Department of Immigration and Citizenship** in Gaborone or Maun.

**Namibia** allows extensions through the **Ministry of Home Affairs and Immigration** in Windhoek, but applications should be submitted well before the visa expires.

## Health & Safety Precautions

Both Botswana and Namibia are generally safe for tourists, but it's important to follow health and safety guidelines to ensure a smooth trip.

### 1. Vaccinations & Health Precautions

**Recommended Vaccinations:**

**Routine vaccinations** (MMR, Tetanus, etc.) should be up to date.

**Hepatitis A & B**: Recommended, especially for travelers staying in rural areas or eating street food.

**Typhoid**: Suggested for travelers planning to stay in more remote areas.

**Malaria Prophylaxis**: Required for some areas, particularly in northern Botswana (e.g., Chobe National Park) during the wet season. Check with your doctor for guidance.

**Yellow Fever**: Required if traveling from a yellow fever-endemic country; not required for travelers coming from non-endemic regions.

**Health & Hygiene Tips:**

**Safe Water**: Drink bottled or purified water to avoid waterborne illnesses.

**Insect Protection**: Use insect repellent (with DEET) to protect against mosquitoes, especially in malaria zones.

**Sun Protection**: The sun can be harsh, so use **high-SPF sunscreen** and wear protective clothing, including a hat.

**Travel Health Kit**: Bring a basic first aid kit, which should include **antiseptic, bandages, pain relievers,** and **anti-diarrheal medication**.

## 2. Safety Tips & Travel Security

**Wildlife Safety:**

Always follow the guidance of your tour guides and park rangers, especially during safaris or hikes.

Keep a safe distance from wild animals, especially in national parks or during game drives.

Be cautious in **remote or desert areas**, as mobile networks can be spotty and rescue services limited.

**General Safety:**

**Street Crime**: While Botswana and Namibia are relatively safe, take basic precautions in cities and towns, such as not leaving valuables unattended and using hotel safes.

**Road Safety**: Roads can be long, remote, and poorly marked, so always drive with caution. Carry extra water, a spare tire, and a map if you plan on self-driving.

**Natural Hazards**: Be aware of extreme temperatures, especially in desert areas. Stay hydrated and avoid being outdoors during the hottest parts of the day (usually noon to 3 p.m.).

## 3. Medical Services

**Botswana** has well-equipped private hospitals in major cities like **Gaborone** and **Maun**, but medical facilities may be limited in remote areas.

**Namibia** offers high-quality health care in **Windhoek**, but **rural areas** may have basic facilities.

It's essential to have **travel insurance** that covers **medical emergencies** and **evacuation** in case of illness or injury.

# Budgeting & Cost Estimates for Botswana & Namibia

Both Botswana and Namibia are renowned for their stunning landscapes and wildlife, but they can be relatively expensive compared to other African destinations. Here's a breakdown of typical costs to help you plan your budget.

## 1. Daily Travel Costs

**Luxury Safari**:

**Accommodation**: $200–$600 per night (high-end lodges or resorts).

**Meals**: $50–$100 per day (fine dining or full-service lodges).

**Activities**: $150–$500 per day (game drives, mokoro rides, private tours).

**Mid-Range Travel**:

**Accommodation**: $80–$200 per night (guesthouses or mid-range lodges).

**Meals**: $20–$50 per day (local restaurants or modest hotels).

**Activities**: $100–$200 per day (guided tours, group safaris).

**Budget Travel**:

**Accommodation**: $20–$50 per night (hostels, camping, or budget guesthouses).

**Meals**: $10–$20 per day (street food, basic cafes, or self-catering).

**Activities**: $50–$100 per day (group tours or self-guided adventures).

## 2. Major Expenses

**Flights**:

Round-trip flights from the **U.S. or Europe** to **Windhoek** (Namibia) or **Gaborone** (Botswana) can cost between **$600–$1,500**, depending on the season.

Regional flights within Botswana or Namibia, such as to **Maun** (for safaris in Botswana) or **Swakopmund** (for coastal adventures in Namibia), can range from **$100–$300** one-way.

**Safari Costs:**

**Guided safaris** in Botswana's **Okavango Delta** or **Chobe National Park** range from **$150–$500 per day** for a group tour. Private safaris and luxury lodges can exceed **$1,000 per day**.

In Namibia, safaris in **Etosha National Park** or **Sossusvlei** typically cost around **$100–$250** for a group tour.

**Car Rentals:**

Renting a **4x4 vehicle** for self-driving can cost **$50–$150 per day**, with additional charges for fuel, insurance, and extra equipment like rooftop tents or GPS.

**Domestic flights** and **transfers** within each country may add extra costs, particularly in remote regions.

### 3. Food & Dining Costs

**Street food** or **local cafes** offer affordable meals for as little as **$5–$10**.

**Mid-range restaurants** in cities or tourist areas may charge **$15–$30** per meal.

**Fine dining** establishments, especially in high-end lodges, may cost **$50–$100** per meal.

### 4. Souvenirs & Shopping

**Local handicrafts** (beaded jewelry, wood carvings, textiles) can range from **$5–$50** depending on the item and its craftsmanship.

**Gems & Jewelry** from Botswana (especially diamonds) or Namibia's **famous Desert Roses** can cost more, with prices varying widely.

### 5. Travel Insurance & Miscellaneous

Comprehensive travel insurance typically costs between **$50–$150** for a **two-week** trip, depending on coverage.

**Tipping** is expected in both countries: typically **10–15%** in restaurants, with small amounts for hotel staff, safari guides, and drivers.

# Best Travel Insurance Options

Travel insurance is essential when visiting Botswana and Namibia, as it ensures you are covered for unexpected events such as medical emergencies, trip cancellations, lost luggage, or travel delays. Here are the best options to consider:

**1. Comprehensive Travel Insurance**

Comprehensive plans cover a wide range of travel mishaps, including trip cancellation, lost luggage, medical emergencies, and more. Many travelers opt for comprehensive policies when visiting Botswana and Namibia due to their remote nature and adventurous activities.

**Top Features to Look For:**

**Medical Coverage**: Emergency medical evacuation, treatment costs, and hospital stays.

**Trip Cancellation/Interruption**: Reimbursement for canceled or interrupted travel due to unforeseen circumstances like illness, family emergencies, or natural disasters.

**Lost Luggage & Personal Belongings**: Reimbursement for lost, stolen, or damaged items.

**24/7 Assistance**: Round-the-clock support in case of emergencies, which is particularly important in remote areas.

**Recommended Providers:**

**World Nomads**: Excellent for adventure travelers; offers coverage for activities like safaris, hiking, and other outdoor sports.

**Allianz Travel Insurance**: Known for reliable customer service and extensive coverage, including medical evacuation and trip interruption.

**Travel Guard**: A solid option with customizable plans to suit different needs, from basic to comprehensive coverage.

## 2. Medical Evacuation Insurance

Due to the remote and rugged nature of Botswana and Namibia, it's essential to have a medical evacuation policy. If you're injured or become ill and need to be airlifted to a hospital, this coverage can save you significant out-of-pocket costs.

**Top Providers:**

**MedJet Assist**: Offers coverage for air medical evacuation to the home country or a medical facility of choice.

**Global Rescue**: Provides both medical evacuation and travel security services, ideal for travelers in remote destinations.

## 3. Adventure & Activity-Specific Insurance

If you plan to engage in adventure activities such as **safaris, hiking, hot air ballooning, or quad biking**, ensure your insurance policy specifically covers these activities. Many general policies exclude high-risk activities, so look for plans that include coverage for outdoor and extreme sports.

**Providers to Consider:**

**World Nomads**: Coverage for a wide variety of adventure activities, including game drives, walking safaris, and more.

**SafetyWing**: A great option for longer-term travelers, covering activities like hiking, trekking, and safaris.

# Transportation: Flights, Buses, and Car Rentals

Getting around Botswana and Namibia can be an adventure in itself, as both countries are vast with many remote areas. Here's what you need to know about your transport options.

### 1. Flights

**International Flights:**

Major international airlines, such as **South African Airways, Qatar Airways,** and **Emirates**, offer flights into both **Windhoek (Namibia)** and **Gaborone (Botswana)**.

Flights from **Europe or the U.S.** to Namibia or Botswana typically take between **15–20 hours** with at least one layover. Expect round-trip fares to range from **$600–$1,500**, depending on the season and booking time.

**Domestic Flights:**

**Botswana**: Major domestic airports include **Maun** (gateway to the Okavango Delta), **Gaborone**, and **Kasane** (for Chobe National Park). Airlines like **Air Botswana** and **Safari Air** provide flights to various destinations within the country.

**Namibia**: Popular domestic flights connect **Windhoek, Swakopmund, Walvis Bay, Etosha**, and **Sossusvlei**. **Air Namibia** and **FlyNamibia** are the primary airlines, with flights starting around **$100–$300** depending on the route.

**Charter Flights:**

**Botswana** and **Namibia** both offer **private charter flights** to remote safari lodges or national parks. These flights are more expensive but provide convenience and flexibility, particularly for safaris in the **Okavango Delta** and **Sossusvlei**.

**2. Buses & Public Transport**

**Botswana:**

Public transportation in Botswana is generally limited to **long-distance buses** and **shared taxis**.

**Intercity buses** are affordable, with routes connecting **Gaborone, Maun, Kasane, and other major towns**. Bus fares are usually **$10–$30** depending on the distance.

**Shared taxis (commonly called "combis")** are available for shorter trips between cities or villages but can be crowded and uncomfortable.

**Namibia:**

**Intercity Buses**: Companies like **Intercape** and **Citi-Link** operate affordable and reliable services between major cities like **Windhoek, Swakopmund, and Walvis Bay**. Fares typically range from **$10–$30** for short distances.

**Local Buses & Taxis**: Taxis are available for short distances in cities like **Windhoek** and **Swakopmund**, though they may not be as readily available outside urban areas.

### 3. Car Rentals & Self-Driving

Self-driving is one of the best ways to explore Botswana and Namibia, especially for those seeking flexibility and the opportunity to visit remote areas at their own pace.

**Rental Cars:**

**4x4 vehicles** are the best option for self-driving in Botswana and Namibia, particularly if you plan to explore national parks or venture into the desert. Rental companies like **Avis**, **Hertz**, and **Europcar** offer these vehicles, with prices typically ranging from **$50–$150 per day**.

Be sure to check if your rental includes **insurance** and **GPS**, especially when driving in remote regions.

**Road Conditions:**

Roads in urban areas are generally paved, but **rural roads** and **game parks** may be gravel or sand, requiring a **4x4** for better handling.

Driving is on the **left-hand side** of the road, and you should always carry **extra water, food, and a spare tire** when heading into remote areas.

**Cross-Border Driving:**

If you plan to drive from **Namibia** to **Botswana** (or vice versa), ensure your car rental includes a **cross-border permit**. Many rental companies charge an additional fee for this service.

### 4. Taxis & Ride-Hailing Services

**Botswana** and **Namibia** have limited options for ride-hailing services like **Uber** or **Bolt**, primarily available in larger cities like **Windhoek** and **Gaborone**.

Traditional taxis are available in urban areas but are not always metered, so it's best to **agree on the fare** before starting the journey.

# Chapter 2: Getting Around

## Domestic Flights & Regional Airlines

Both Botswana and Namibia offer domestic flights that can help you cover long distances quickly, especially to remote and popular destinations. Here's what you need to know about flying within both countries:

**Botswana**

**Air Botswana**: The national carrier offers regular flights connecting major cities like **Gaborone**, **Maun**, **Kasane**, and **Francistown**. Flights to **Maun** and **Kasane** are popular for travelers heading to **Okavango Delta** and **Chobe National Park**.

**Flight Time**: Short flights within Botswana range from 1 to 2 hours.

**Price Range**: One-way flights are typically priced between **$80 and $200** depending on the destination.

**Safari Air**: A smaller regional airline, primarily offering chartered flights to remote locations, including safaris in national parks. Safari Air is ideal if you're looking to go beyond the usual tourist spots.

**Regional Airlines**:

**Air Namibia**: Provides flights to and from Namibia's major cities, like **Windhoek**, **Swakopmund**, and **Etosha National Park**.

**FlyNamibia**: A reliable domestic carrier servicing smaller towns and airports within Namibia, including routes to **Swakopmund** and **Walvis Bay**.

**Flight Time**: Domestic flights usually range from **1 to 2 hours**.

**Price Range**: Tickets generally cost between **$60 to $150** per flight.

# Public Transport: Buses & Shared Taxis

Public transportation in Botswana and Namibia is relatively basic, but it's still a good option for budget-conscious travelers or those looking for local experiences. Here's a breakdown of what to expect:

## Botswana

**Intercity Buses**:

Long-distance buses in Botswana are affordable and often operate on a scheduled basis between major cities like **Gaborone**, **Maun**, and **Kasane**.

Companies like **Naledi and Intercape** provide services for both domestic and cross-border routes.

**Price Range**: Bus fares typically range from **$10 to $30** depending on the distance.

**Travel Time**: Depending on the route, bus trips can last anywhere from 4 to 8 hours.

**Shared Taxis (Combis)**:

Known locally as **combis**, these shared taxis are typically minivans that follow specific routes within urban areas and between cities.

**Price Range**: Typically cheaper than buses, with fares starting at **$2 to $5** for short trips within cities.

**Convenience**: While affordable, combis can be crowded and may not be the most comfortable way to travel.

## Namibia

**Intercity Buses**:

**Intercape** and **Citi-Link** are the primary intercity bus companies offering services throughout Namibia.

**Price Range**: Bus fares generally range from **$10 to $40**, depending on the distance and service class.

**Popular Routes**: Major routes include **Windhoek to Swakopmund, Windhoek to Walvis Bay**, and **Windhoek to Etosha**.

**Travel Time**: Bus journeys can take anywhere from 3 to 6 hours, depending on the route.

**Local Buses and Shared Taxis**:

**Taxis** are available in cities like **Windhoek, Swakopmund**, and **Walvis Bay**, and they operate on an unofficial basis. Expect to share the ride with others traveling along the same route.

**Price Range**: Short-distance taxis typically cost **$2 to $5** per trip, but the price can vary depending on the distance.

## Self-Driving Tips & Road Conditions

Self-driving is one of the best ways to explore Botswana and Namibia, especially for adventurous travelers looking to access remote areas, national parks, and breathtaking landscapes. However, driving in these countries requires some preparation and awareness of local road conditions.

**Self-Driving Tips**

**Drive on the Left**: Both Botswana and Namibia follow the left-hand side of the road. Ensure you're comfortable with this before setting off.

**Rent a 4x4**: Many of the most popular destinations, including national parks and safari areas, are only accessible by **4x4 vehicles**. Opt for a rental vehicle with high clearance, especially if you plan to visit more remote regions.

**Carry Essentials**: Always have extra water, food, fuel, and a spare tire when driving in remote areas. Fuel stations can be few and far between in rural regions.

**Driving Hours**: Most roads are in good condition, but if you're venturing off the main highways, driving at night is not recommended due to wildlife crossing the roads and limited lighting.

**Speed Limits**: Speed limits in urban areas are typically around **50 km/h** (31 mph), and on highways, it's around **120 km/h** (74 mph). Always adhere to posted speed limits, and be cautious when passing through rural areas or villages.

**Insurance**: Ensure that your rental vehicle is covered by insurance, including **third-party insurance** for damage or accidents. Verify that the coverage includes driving in remote areas.

**Road Signs & Navigation**: Road signs are generally well-marked, but be prepared for a lack of signage in more rural areas. Using **GPS or offline maps** (such as Google Maps) is highly recommended.

### Road Conditions

**Paved Roads**: Major cities like **Gaborone** (Botswana) and **Windhoek** (Namibia) have paved roads and highways in good condition. Routes between larger cities and key tourist destinations are typically well-maintained.

**Gravel & Dirt Roads**: Many of the popular safari areas and remote locations (such as the **Okavango Delta** or **Sossusvlei**) are accessible via gravel roads. These roads may be **dusty, bumpy**, and in some cases, muddy depending on the weather.

**Sand Dunes**: In places like **Sossusvlei** (Namibia) and parts of Botswana's **Kalahari Desert**, expect **sand roads**. A **4x4 vehicle** is necessary to handle the soft sand. Driving in sand can be tricky; if you get stuck, stay calm and deflate your tires slightly for better traction.

## Border Crossings & Customs Regulations

Crossing the border between Botswana and Namibia (or any neighboring countries) is relatively straightforward but requires familiarity with customs regulations and proper documentation.

### Border Crossings

**Popular Border Crossings**:

**Kasane (Botswana) to Namibia's Caprivi Strip**: Easily accessible and commonly used by travelers moving between Botswana's **Chobe National Park** and Namibia's **Caprivi Strip**.

**Ngoma Border Post (Botswana) to Namibia**: A popular crossing point between **Chobe** and the **Zambezi Region** in Namibia.

**Mamuno (Botswana) to Namibia**: Another entry point that connects the **Kgalagadi Transfrontier Park** (Botswana) and **Namibian desert regions**.

**Travel Tips**:

**Wait Time**: Be prepared for potential delays, especially during peak travel seasons. Border posts can get busy, so plan accordingly and bring some snacks and drinks.

**Hours of Operation**: Most border posts are open from **6:00 AM to 10:00 PM**, but it's always best to check ahead, especially during public holidays or weekends.

## Customs Regulations

**Documents Required**:

**Passport**: Ensure that your passport is valid for at least **six months** beyond your planned return date.

**Visa**: Verify visa requirements for both Botswana and Namibia before traveling. For many nationalities, a visa may be required for either or both countries.

**Vehicle Permit**: If you're driving your own car or renting one, you will need to obtain a **temporary import permit** for the vehicle at the border. This is typically valid for **30 to 90 days**.

**Insurance**: Proof of **third-party insurance** is required when driving a vehicle across the border. You can usually purchase this at the border post.

**Duty-Free Allowance**:

Travelers are typically allowed to bring in **personal items** duty-free, such as clothing and cameras, as long as they are not for commercial purposes.

Be mindful of the **alcohol** and **tobacco** limits as well, as customs may impose restrictions on the quantities you can carry across borders.

**Customs Declarations**:

Declare any **items** that may be restricted or valuable, such as **electronic devices, large amounts of cash**, or **protected animal products**.

**Agricultural Products**: Many countries in Southern Africa, including Botswana and Namibia, have restrictions on the importation of agricultural products (especially fruits, vegetables, or plants) to prevent the spread of diseases.

**Pets**: If traveling with pets, ensure that you have the appropriate veterinary certificates, rabies vaccination records, and permits for your pet to cross the border.

By planning ahead and adhering to these tips, border crossings can be smooth, and you can focus on enjoying your adventure through Botswana and Namibia.

## Travel Apps & Navigation Tools

When traveling through Botswana and Namibia, having reliable travel apps and navigation tools is essential, especially in remote areas where access to physical maps may be limited. Here are some useful apps and tools to make your trip more seamless:

### 1. Google Maps

**Purpose**: Essential for navigation, Google Maps works well in cities and some rural areas. It's useful for finding accommodations, restaurants, and tourist attractions.

**Offline Features**: You can download maps for offline use in areas with limited internet connectivity, which is especially helpful in remote locations like national parks.

### 2. Maps.me

**Purpose**: A great offline map app that offers detailed maps for Botswana and Namibia. This app is perfect for navigating areas where network coverage may be unreliable.

**Offline Features**: Fully functional offline, Maps.me allows you to download regions and track your location without data.

### 3. Safari Live

**Purpose**: If you're planning on safaris, **Safari Live** is an excellent app for real-time updates from safari guides and wildlife enthusiasts. It provides location-based wildlife sightings and is ideal for use in popular safari areas like the **Okavango Delta** and **Chobe National Park**.

**Offline Features**: Includes safari-specific tips and maps, though live updates require a data connection.

### 4. iOverlander

**Purpose**: This app provides detailed information on campsites, restaurants, accommodations, and other essential travel resources. It's ideal for self-drivers and overlanders.

**Offline Features**: You can download locations and details to access offline.

### 5. XE Currency

**Purpose**: Currency conversion is often needed, especially when crossing borders. **XE Currency** is a reliable tool to help you understand exchange rates between different currencies, such as Namibian dollars, Botswanan pula, and international currencies.

**Offline Features**: The app allows you to check rates offline after downloading them.

### 6. WhatsApp

**Purpose**: WhatsApp is the most common messaging app in both Botswana and Namibia, used for communicating with local guides, hosts, and fellow travelers.

**Internet Access**: WhatsApp works over Wi-Fi or mobile data, which can be a bit scarce in remote regions.

### 7. TripAdvisor

**Purpose**: Use TripAdvisor to read reviews on restaurants, accommodations, and attractions. It's a helpful tool for planning your day-to-day itinerary, especially when visiting popular tourist spots.

**Offline Features**: Some reviews and information can be saved for offline use.

### 8. Sygic Travel

**Purpose**: This app is great for creating customized itineraries and maps. It has preloaded guides for Botswana and Namibia, which include top attractions, restaurants, and accommodations.

**Offline Features**: The app allows you to download maps and itineraries to access offline.

# Chapter 3: Where to Stay

## Luxury Lodges & Resorts

Luxury hotels in Botswana and Namibia offer an exclusive and unforgettable experience for tourists seeking comfort, elegance, and top-notch service. These accommodations provide exceptional amenities, stunning locations, and personalized services, ensuring a memorable stay for those exploring the beauty of Southern Africa. Whether nestled in the heart of the desert or overlooking majestic wildlife, luxury hotels create the perfect environment for relaxation and adventure.

1. **San Camp - Botswana**

San Camp is an exclusive, remote luxury camp located in the heart of the Makgadikgadi Salt Pans in Botswana. It is ideal for those looking for a unique and serene experience surrounded by the vast wilderness, offering a sense of peace and quiet unlike any other.

**Location (Address & Proximity):**

San Camp is located on the edge of the Makgadikgadi Salt Pans, which are some of the largest salt pans in the world. It is accessible via light aircraft flights from Maun Airport, approximately a 30-minute flight.

**Highlights:**

Breathtaking views of the salt pans and desert.

Interaction with San Bushmen for cultural immersion.

Elephant, zebra, and wildebeest sightings in the dry season.

Salt pan excursions and quad biking.

Stargazing in an area with clear, unobstructed skies.

**Spa and Wellness:**

San Camp doesn't have a formal spa, but it offers relaxing wellness experiences like private massages in serene, scenic spots around the camp.

**Bars:**

There is an intimate bar area where guests can enjoy drinks while taking in the stunning desert scenery.

**Events and Conferences:**

San Camp is not geared toward large events or conferences due to its remote location and boutique nature. It caters to smaller, intimate groups and private getaways.

**Basic Facilities and Amenities:**

Luxury tents with en-suite bathrooms.

Solar-powered electricity.

Wi-Fi in the central area.

Hot and cold running water.

Gourmet dining.

A small boutique offering local crafts.

**Opening and Closing Hours:**

The camp operates seasonally from April to November.

**Price:**

Prices range from $900 to $1,200 per night depending on the season and type of accommodation.

**Pros:**

Remote, exclusive location.

Unique experiences like quad biking and cultural immersion.

Stunning scenery and wildlife encounters.

Intimate, personalized service.

**Cons:**

Limited to smaller groups.

Remote location may not appeal to everyone.

**Local Tips:**

If you're traveling during the rainy season, be prepared for muddy roads and seasonal closures.

For a unique experience, visit during the green season (December to March) to witness the migration of animals.

## 2. The Royal Tree Lodge - Namibia

Nestled in the Zambezi region of Namibia, The Royal Tree Lodge offers an exceptional experience of luxury combined with a deep immersion in nature. This lodge provides a tranquil escape into the wild with outstanding service and a beautiful location.

**Location (Address & Proximity):**

Located in the Zambezi region, it's approximately 10 km from the nearest town, Katima Mulilo, and 40 km from the Namibia-Zambia border.

**Highlights:**

Overlooks the Zambezi River, providing panoramic views.

Opportunity for boat safaris and bird watching.

A range of game activities, including guided walks and game drives.

Scenic sundowners overlooking the river.

**Spa and Wellness:**

The lodge has a small wellness area with a focus on relaxation and rejuvenation, offering massages and treatments for ultimate relaxation.

**Bars:**
There is a sophisticated bar serving a selection of international and local drinks. The riverside bar offers a great atmosphere for sunset views.

**Events and Conferences:**

The lodge is well-equipped for small meetings and events with a designated conference room that has modern AV equipment and internet access.

**Basic Facilities and Amenities:**

Luxury tents with private decks.

En-suite bathrooms with modern amenities.

Outdoor pool.

Free Wi-Fi in common areas.

Laundry service.

Dining with local specialties.

**Opening and Closing Hours:**

The lodge operates year-round, with some seasonal closures in the rainy season (December to March).

**Price:**
Rates range from $600 to $1,000 per night per person, depending on the season and room type.

**Pros:**

Beautiful riverside location with easy access to river-based activities.

Offers a mix of luxury and nature experiences.

Excellent service and personalized attention.

**Cons:**

The lodge can be expensive during peak season.

Limited activities compared to larger resorts.

**Local Tips:**

Visit the lodge during the dry season (May to October) for the best wildlife viewing and river activities.

Book early for river safaris, as they fill up quickly.

### 3. Zannier Hotels Sonop - Namibia

Zannier Hotels Sonop is a lavish, tented camp located in the heart of the Namib Desert. The resort combines modern luxury with a rugged desert environment, offering guests a chance to immerse themselves in one of the world's most stunning landscapes.

**Location (Address & Proximity):**

Located near the Namib Desert, Sonop is situated about 100 km from Sossusvlei, making it a perfect base for exploring the famous dunes.

**Highlights:**

Panoramic views of the desert and nearby mountains.

Beautifully designed tents with private pools.

Guided desert excursions including dune climbing and stargazing.

Hot air ballooning.

**Spa and Wellness:**

The spa offers treatments inspired by the desert, such as stone massages and detoxifying therapies, as well as a sauna and outdoor plunge pool.

**Bars:**
There is a stylish bar with a wide selection of wines, cocktails, and spirits. The bar area offers stunning views of the desert landscape.

**Events and Conferences:**

The resort caters to corporate groups and private events, with luxury conference facilities and event spaces.

**Basic Facilities and Amenities:**

Luxury tents with king-size beds and plunge pools.

Air conditioning and Wi-Fi in common areas.

Exclusive dining with a focus on local ingredients.

Helicopter pad.

Pool and wellness center.

**Opening and Closing Hours:**

Zannier Hotels Sonop operates year-round.

**Price:**
Prices start at approximately $1,200 per night per person.

**Pros:**

A stunning desert location with incredible views.

Luxurious tents with modern amenities.

Exclusive and remote experience with plenty of outdoor activities.

**Cons:**

High price point may not be affordable for all.

Limited access to nearby towns and cities.

**Local Tips:**

Bring light, breathable clothing for the day and warm clothes for the evenings, as the desert temperature can vary dramatically.

### 4. Chobe Game Lodge - Botswana

Chobe Game Lodge is located in the Chobe National Park, Botswana's most famous national park, known for its large elephant population. It combines luxury and nature with access to the Chobe River and world-class game viewing.

**Location (Address & Proximity):**

Located within Chobe National Park, the lodge is approximately 10 km from Kasane and accessible by both road and air.

**Highlights:**

Access to Chobe River and boat safaris.

Rich wildlife including elephants, lions, and buffalo.

Walking safaris and game drives.

Beautiful sunset views from the river.

**Spa and Wellness:**
The lodge offers a spa with various wellness treatments including massages and body scrubs. There's also a fitness center for those looking to stay active.

**Bars:**
There's a lively bar with great views of the river, perfect for enjoying a drink during sunset.

**Events and Conferences:**

Chobe Game Lodge has facilities for small conferences and events, equipped with AV systems and Wi-Fi.

**Basic Facilities and Amenities:**

Luxury suites with river views.

Wi-Fi in public areas.

Swimming pool and fitness center.

Gourmet restaurant.

Laundry and concierge services.

**Opening and Closing Hours:**

Chobe Game Lodge operates year-round.

**Price:**
Prices start at $700 per night per person.

**Pros:**

Fantastic wildlife experiences with the chance to see the "Big Five."

Excellent service and accommodations.

River-based activities and luxury game drives.

**Cons:**

The lodge can get crowded during peak seasons.

Prices can be high compared to other options.

**Local Tips:**

Book a boat safari early in the morning or late in the evening for the best wildlife sightings.

### 5. Wolwedans Dunes Lodge - Namibia

Wolwedans Dunes Lodge offers an intimate experience set in the heart of the NamibRand Nature Reserve, providing a peaceful retreat in a breathtaking desert landscape. The lodge is known for its eco-luxury accommodations and eco-tourism practices.

**Location (Address & Proximity):**

Located within the NamibRand Nature Reserve, about 90 km from Sesriem and Sossusvlei, the lodge is accessible by light aircraft or a scenic drive from nearby areas.

**Highlights:**

Stunning views of the Namib Desert and towering dunes.

Private desert drives and walks with expert guides.

Sustainable practices integrated into the resort's operations.

Photography opportunities in the early morning light.

**Spa and Wellness:**

The lodge offers a tranquil wellness experience with massages and holistic treatments in a serene desert setting.

**Bars:**
There's an open-air bar with panoramic views of the desert, perfect for unwinding after a day of activities.

**Events and Conferences:**

Wolwedans is suitable for small gatherings and private events, offering customized event planning services.

**Basic Facilities and Amenities:**

Eco-friendly chalets and luxury tents.

En-suite bathrooms with outdoor showers.

Solar-powered facilities.

Complimentary Wi-Fi in common areas.

Gourmet dining with fresh, local ingredients.

**Opening and Closing Hours:**

The lodge operates year-round.

**Price:**
Prices range from $500 to $850 per night depending on the season.

**Pros:**

Sustainable luxury in a pristine desert environment.

Remote and peaceful location with few tourists.

Excellent service and high-end accommodations.

**Cons:**

Remote location means limited activities outside of the lodge.

Higher price during peak seasons.

**Local Tips:**

Take a morning walk or drive to experience the desert at its most tranquil and to capture the early light.

# Mid-Range Hotels & Guesthouses

Mid-range hotels and guesthouses in Botswana and Namibia offer a balance of comfort, quality, and affordability. These accommodations provide cozy rooms, reliable amenities, and a welcoming atmosphere, making them ideal for tourists who want a great experience without the high-end price tag. Located in key areas, they offer convenient access to popular attractions while maintaining a relaxed and friendly environment. Perfect for those seeking value and comfort during their Southern African adventure.

1. **Thakadu River Camp - Botswana**

Thakadu River Camp is located in the Northern part of Botswana, near the Khwai River. It offers a charming mix of comfort and authentic wilderness, making it a perfect spot for wildlife lovers and those seeking a more affordable safari experience.

**Location (Address & Proximity):**

Located in the Khwai Community Area, about 35 km from the Moremi Game Reserve, and accessible by 4x4 vehicles or light aircraft from Maun Airport.

**Highlights:**

Scenic views of the Khwai River and surrounding bush.

Wildlife viewing including elephants, hippos, and various bird species.

Guided safari tours and nature walks.

River activities such as canoeing and fishing.

**Spa and Wellness:**

While Thakadu River Camp does not offer a full-fledged spa, they provide in-room massages and wellness treatments on request.

**Bars:**

The lodge features a cozy bar area with a selection of wines, beers, and cocktails, often enjoyed by guests as they relax by the river.

**Events and Conferences:**

Thakadu River Camp is better suited for smaller group retreats or intimate gatherings rather than large conferences.

**Basic Facilities and Amenities:**

Comfortable safari tents with private bathrooms.

Wi-Fi available in the main lodge area.

Outdoor pool.

Gift shop with local crafts.

In-house dining with a menu focused on local cuisine.

**Opening and Closing Hours:**

The lodge is open year-round, with seasonal changes in availability due to weather.

**Price:**
Prices range from $300 to $500 per night per person, depending on the season and type of accommodation.

**Pros:**

Affordable luxury compared to high-end safari lodges.

Fantastic location for game viewing and proximity to Moremi.

Friendly, knowledgeable staff.

**Cons:**

Limited luxury amenities compared to higher-end options.

The camp can get busy during peak season.

**Local Tips:**

Bring along binoculars for birdwatching, as the area is rich with birdlife.

For the best wildlife sightings, visit during the dry season (May to October).

## 2. The Elegant Guesthouse - Namibia

The Elegant Guesthouse in Windhoek offers modern, stylish accommodations in the heart of Namibia's capital city. It's perfect for travelers who want to experience the urban side of Namibia, with easy access to shopping, dining, and attractions.

**Location (Address & Proximity):**

Located in central Windhoek, about 45 minutes from Hosea Kutako International Airport.

**Highlights:**

Central location near major city attractions like the Independence Memorial Museum and Christ Church.

Easy access to restaurants, shops, and local culture.

Contemporary, elegant design with spacious rooms.

**Spa and Wellness:**

The guesthouse offers wellness services such as massages and a sauna for relaxation after a day of sightseeing.

**Bars:**
An on-site bar offers a range of beverages including local wines, spirits, and cocktails. It is a good place to unwind after a day in Windhoek.

**Events and Conferences:**

The Elegant Guesthouse has a small conference room equipped for business meetings and small events.

**Basic Facilities and Amenities:**

Air-conditioned rooms with en-suite bathrooms.

Free Wi-Fi and flat-screen TVs.

Swimming pool and fitness center.

Airport transfers available.

Breakfast included in the stay.

**Opening and Closing Hours:**
The guesthouse operates year-round, and check-in/check-out times are flexible based on guest needs.

**Price:**
Prices range from $120 to $180 per night for a double room.

**Pros:**

Central location with easy access to Windhoek's attractions.

Affordable yet stylish accommodations.

Excellent customer service.

**Cons:**

Limited space and facilities for large events or extended stays.

Can be noisy due to the city center location.

**Local Tips:**

Explore the local markets for souvenirs, such as the Namibia Craft Centre.

Take a walking tour of Windhoek to learn more about the city's history.

### 3. Eagle's Nest Lodge - Namibia

Situated in the heart of the Namib Desert, Eagle's Nest Lodge offers a tranquil escape with stunning views of the surrounding mountains and dunes. This guesthouse-style lodge is ideal for nature lovers who seek comfort and convenience in a serene setting.

**Location (Address & Proximity):**

Located about 25 km from the town of Solitaire and 250 km from Sossusvlei, the lodge is easily accessible by 4x4 vehicles.

**Highlights:**

Spectacular views of the desert landscape and distant mountains.

Hiking trails and guided excursions.

Close proximity to Sossusvlei and the famous dunes.

Eco-friendly lodge with solar energy and water conservation practices.

**Spa and Wellness:**

While the lodge does not have a dedicated spa, they offer wellness services, including yoga classes and guided meditation sessions for relaxation.

**Bars:**
The lodge has a small but well-stocked bar, ideal for enjoying sundowners while taking in the desert views.

**Events and Conferences:**

The lodge has a small, intimate meeting space perfect for private events or corporate retreats.

**Basic Facilities and Amenities:**

Comfortable rooms and tented chalets with modern amenities.

Outdoor pool.

Free Wi-Fi in common areas.

Restaurant serving Namibian and international dishes.

Laundry services.

**Opening and Closing Hours:**

Eagle's Nest Lodge operates year-round.

**Price:**
Rates range from $150 to $250 per night depending on the season.

**Pros:**

Stunning desert views and quiet surroundings.

Great for nature lovers and those seeking relaxation.

Eco-friendly practices.

**Cons:**

Can feel isolated, especially for those seeking more urban amenities.

Limited activities in the immediate area outside of nature exploration.

**Local Tips:**

Visit the nearby Sossusvlei dunes at sunrise for the best photo opportunities.

Bring warm clothing, as desert temperatures can drop significantly at night.

### 4. Chobe Safari Lodge - Botswana

Situated on the banks of the Chobe River, Chobe Safari Lodge offers mid-range accommodation with a variety of activities, from river safaris to game drives. It's an excellent base for exploring Chobe National Park and its rich wildlife.

**Location (Address & Proximity):**

Located in Kasane, Botswana, near Chobe National Park, and about 10 km from the Kazungula border with Zimbabwe and Zambia.

**Highlights:**

River safaris and game drives in Chobe National Park.

Stunning views of the river and surrounding wildlife.

Elephant and lion sightings are common in the area.

Variety of accommodation options including luxury tents and chalets.

**Spa and Wellness:**

The lodge features a small wellness area offering spa treatments, including massages and body wraps.

**Bars:**

There is a riverside bar where guests can relax with a drink while watching the sunset and wildlife along the Chobe River.

**Events and Conferences:**

The lodge offers event and conference facilities suitable for small to medium-sized groups, with modern AV equipment and catering services.

**Basic Facilities and Amenities:**

Comfortable rooms with en-suite bathrooms.

Restaurant offering international and local cuisine.

Free Wi-Fi in public areas.

Outdoor pool.

**Opening and Closing Hours:**

Chobe Safari Lodge is open year-round.

**Price:**
Prices range from $120 to $300 per night, depending on the season and type of accommodation.

**Pros:**

Great location for wildlife viewing and exploring Chobe National Park.

Range of activities, from safaris to boat trips.

Relaxed atmosphere with excellent service.

**Cons:**

Can get crowded, especially during peak tourist seasons.

Some areas of the lodge may show signs of wear and tear.

**Local Tips:**

Book game drives and boat safaris in advance to secure your spot.

Bring mosquito repellent, as the area is near wetlands.

## 5. Chalene Guest House - Namibia

**Overview:**

Chalene Guest House is located in the tranquil town of Swakopmund, offering modern amenities with the charm of a guesthouse. Ideal for those seeking a relaxing stop on the Namibian coast with access to both the beach and desert adventures.

**Location (Address & Proximity):**

Located in Swakopmund, 35 km from Walvis Bay Airport and a short walk from the beach.

**Highlights:**

Close proximity to Swakopmund's attractions like the Swakopmund Museum, and desert excursions.

A family-friendly environment with spacious rooms.

A calm oasis after a day of exploring the coastal region.

**Spa and Wellness:**

The guesthouse offers a small wellness area with massages and relaxation treatments upon request.

**Bars:**

Chalene Guest House has an on-site bar serving a selection of beverages, perfect for relaxing after a day of activities.

**Events and Conferences:**

The guesthouse is not specifically set up for large events or conferences but can accommodate smaller groups for meetings.

**Basic Facilities and Amenities:**

Comfortable rooms with en-suite bathrooms.

Wi-Fi and satellite TV.

Breakfast included.

Outdoor patio and garden.

Airport transfers available.

**Opening and Closing Hours:**

Chalene Guest House operates year-round, with flexible check-in and check-out times.

**Price:**
Prices range from $80 to $150 per night for a double room.

**Pros:**

Convenient location in Swakopmund.

Affordable with excellent service.

Great for families or small groups.

**Cons:**

Limited facilities for larger events or corporate groups.

The guesthouse's small size can make it feel busy during peak season.

**Local Tips:**

Take a dune tour in the nearby Namib Desert for an exhilarating experience.

Explore the Swakopmund waterfront for great dining and souvenir shopping.

# Budget-Friendly Hostels & Campsites

Budget-friendly hostels and campsites in Botswana and Namibia offer affordable options for travelers seeking a more rustic and adventurous experience. These accommodations provide basic but comfortable facilities, perfect for those looking to save money while exploring the natural beauty of the region. Whether staying in a lively hostel or camping under the stars, guests can enjoy the outdoors and connect with fellow travelers, all while experiencing the unique landscapes and wildlife of Southern Africa.

### 1. Backpacker's Choice - Windhoek, Namibia

Backpacker's Choice in Windhoek is a popular, budget-friendly hostel that attracts backpackers and solo travelers from all over the world. It's located in a convenient part of Namibia's capital, providing affordable accommodations with a social and welcoming atmosphere.

**Location (Address & Proximity):**

Located in the heart of Windhoek, approximately 45 minutes from Hosea Kutako International Airport. Close to shops, restaurants, and other urban attractions.

**Highlights:**

Social atmosphere ideal for meeting other travelers.

Central location with easy access to major attractions in Windhoek.

Free Wi-Fi and communal kitchen for self-catering.

Organized city tours and excursions.

**Spa and Wellness:**

The hostel does not offer spa services, but guests can enjoy a relaxed outdoor garden area for unwinding.

**Bars:**

There is no dedicated bar, but the hostel has a lounge area where guests can socialize and enjoy beverages.

**Events and Conferences:**

Backpacker's Choice is mainly focused on individual travelers, so it does not cater to large events or conferences.

**Basic Facilities and Amenities:**

Dormitory and private rooms.

Free Wi-Fi.

Shared kitchen facilities.

Secure luggage storage.

Laundry services.

**Opening and Closing Hours:**

Open year-round, with check-in and check-out times flexible based on availability.

**Price:**
Dormitory beds start at approximately $15 per night, while private rooms range from $40 to $60.

**Pros:**

Very affordable for budget travelers.

Social atmosphere and opportunity to meet other backpackers.

Great central location in Windhoek.

**Cons:**

Limited privacy in dormitory rooms.

Basic amenities; lacks luxury comforts.

**Local Tips:**

Use the communal kitchen to prepare meals and save on food costs.

Take a walking tour of Windhoek to explore the city and its history.

## 2. Chobe River Campsite - Botswana

Chobe River Campsite is a budget-friendly campsite located in the Chobe National Park, Botswana. It provides an affordable way to explore the park's wildlife without the cost of staying at luxury lodges. The campsite is set in a stunning location, right next to the Chobe River.

**Location (Address & Proximity):**

Located in the Chobe National Park, 5 km from Kasane, and about 80 km from the Victoria Falls. The campsite is easily accessible by road and also offers easy access to game drives.

**Highlights:**

Proximity to the Chobe River and Chobe National Park.

Excellent wildlife sightings, including elephants, lions, and buffalo.

Guided game drives and boat safaris available.

Beautiful sunset views over the Chobe River.

**Spa and Wellness:**

No formal spa services available, but the campsite offers a relaxed outdoor atmosphere perfect for unwinding after a day of activities.

**Bars:**
There is a small camp bar where guests can enjoy refreshing drinks after a long day of wildlife activities.

**Events and Conferences:**

Chobe River Campsite is not designed for conferences or large events, but it is suitable for group camping experiences.

**Basic Facilities and Amenities:**

Basic camping facilities with designated tented areas.

Shared restrooms and showers.

BBQ facilities for self-catering.

Small bar and outdoor dining area.

Free Wi-Fi in public areas.

**Opening and Closing Hours:**

Open year-round, although peak season tends to be from May to October.

**Price:**
Tent sites start at approximately $10 to $15 per person per night.

**Pros:**

Excellent location for game viewing and river activities.

Affordable for those wanting to experience Chobe without high costs.

Great for nature lovers and wildlife enthusiasts.

**Cons:**

Basic facilities compared to higher-end campsites or lodges.

Can get busy during peak seasons.

**Local Tips:**

Bring your own camping gear, though basic equipment is available to rent.

Arrive early in the day to secure a good spot, as the campsite can fill up during peak seasons.

### 3. Swakopmund Backpackers - Namibia

Swakopmund Backpackers is a vibrant and affordable hostel located in the coastal town of Swakopmund. Known for its welcoming environment, it's a great base for travelers who want to explore both the desert and the coast of Namibia.

**Location (Address & Proximity):**

Located in the heart of Swakopmund, only a short walk from the beach and major town attractions. It's approximately 400 km from Windhoek.

**Highlights:**

Close to the beach, dunes, and adventure activities such as sandboarding and quad biking.

Cozy and relaxed environment perfect for solo travelers and small groups.

Daily tours to nearby attractions, including the desert and Skeleton Coast.

**Spa and Wellness:**

There are no spa facilities on-site, but guests can unwind in the communal lounge area or explore the nearby beaches for a relaxing experience.

**Bars:**
A small bar area is available where guests can enjoy drinks and socialize with other travelers.

**Events and Conferences:**

Swakopmund Backpackers is primarily for travelers looking for a casual stay, and it doesn't have formal conference facilities.

**Basic Facilities and Amenities:**

Dormitory and private rooms available.

Shared kitchen for self-catering.

Free Wi-Fi in common areas.

Lounge and outdoor seating area.

Laundry service.

**Opening and Closing Hours:**

The hostel is open year-round, with check-in/check-out times between 12 pm and 10 pm.

**Price:**
Dormitory beds range from $12 to $18 per night, while private rooms are available from $35 to $50 per night.

**Pros:**

Great social atmosphere with plenty of opportunities to meet other travelers.

Convenient location for exploring Swakopmund and surrounding areas.

Low-cost accommodation with clean facilities.

**Cons:**

Basic amenities and shared facilities.

Can be noisy, especially during peak season.

**Local Tips:**

Take advantage of the hostel's partnerships for discounts on adventure activities.

Visit the nearby desert for scenic dunes and photography opportunities.

### 4. Okavango River Campsite - Botswana

The Okavango River Campsite offers budget-friendly camping options on the banks of the Okavango River, providing an excellent base for exploring the Okavango Delta and surrounding areas. The site is perfect for those looking for an affordable yet immersive wildlife experience.

**Location (Address & Proximity):**

Located near the town of Shakawe, along the Okavango River. It's accessible by road and provides easy access to the Okavango Delta and local fishing spots.

**Highlights:**

Fantastic wildlife sightings, including birds and aquatic animals.

Fishing and boat trips available along the Okavango River.

Stunning views of the river and delta.

Proximity to the UNESCO-listed Okavango Delta, ideal for wildlife and bird watching.

**Spa and Wellness:**

No spa services available, but the natural setting and peaceful surroundings offer a rejuvenating experience.

**Bars:**

The campsite has a small bar area where travelers can enjoy drinks while watching the sunset over the river.

**Events and Conferences:**

Not designed for large conferences, but suitable for small group retreats or private camping experiences.

**Basic Facilities and Amenities:**

Basic campsites with clean, shared facilities.

Self-catering kitchen.

River access for boat and fishing activities.

Limited Wi-Fi access.

**Opening and Closing Hours:**

Open year-round, with peak season from May to October.

**Price:**

Prices range from $8 to $15 per person per night for camping.

**Pros:**

Great location for wildlife viewing and river activities.

Affordable for backpackers and campers.

Beautiful, peaceful environment for nature lovers.

**Cons:**

Basic amenities, which may not suit everyone.

Limited access to modern conveniences.

**Local Tips:**

Bring your own fishing equipment if you plan to fish in the river.

Book boat tours in advance, as they are popular with visitors.

### 5. Sesriem Campsite - Namibia

Located near the famous Sossusvlei dunes, Sesriem Campsite is the perfect base for exploring the Namib Desert on a budget. Managed by Namibia Wildlife Resorts, it offers simple yet comfortable camping accommodations with excellent access to one of Namibia's top attractions.

**Location (Address & Proximity):**

Situated in the Namib-Naukluft National Park, about 5 km from the entrance to Sossusvlei. The campsite is accessible by road from Windhoek.

**Highlights:**

Close proximity to Sossusvlei, one of the world's most iconic desert destinations.

Stunning desert views and starry nights.

Safe and well-maintained campsite with shared facilities.

Great for exploring the nearby dunes and Deadvlei.

**Spa and Wellness:**

No spa facilities, but the tranquility of the desert makes for a relaxing environment.

**Bars:**
There is a small on-site shop and bar, where guests can purchase drinks and snacks.

**Events and Conferences:**

The campsite is more for individual travelers and small groups rather than large events.

**Basic Facilities and Amenities:**

Basic campsites with access to shared restrooms and showers.

Self-catering kitchen and braai (BBQ) facilities.

Limited Wi-Fi.

**Opening and Closing Hours:**

The campsite is open year-round.

**Price:**
Rates range from $10 to $20 per person per night.

**Pros:**

Affordable accommodation near the iconic Sossusvlei dunes.

Great for early morning photography and desert exploration.

Well-maintained and secure campsite.

**Cons:**

Basic facilities compared to lodges or hotels.

Can be crowded during peak tourist season.

**Local Tips:**

Arrive early to get a good camping spot, especially during high season.

Don't miss the sunrise at Sossusvlei; it's one of the most beautiful sights in Namibia.

# Unique Stays: Safari Camps & Desert Lodges

Unique stays like safari camps and desert lodges in Botswana and Namibia provide an unforgettable experience for travelers looking to immerse themselves in nature. These accommodations offer a chance to stay close to wildlife in the heart of game reserves or experience the vast, serene beauty of desert landscapes. With luxurious tented camps or remote lodges, guests can enjoy guided safaris, star-gazing, and unparalleled views, all while embracing the tranquility and adventure of Southern Africa's wilderness.

1. Sanctuary Chief's Camp - Botswana

Sanctuary Chief's Camp is one of Botswana's most renowned luxury safari camps, situated in the Okavango Delta's Moremi Game Reserve. It offers an exclusive, luxurious safari experience with excellent game viewing and a chance to see the Big Five in a pristine, remote setting.

**Location (Address & Proximity):**

Located on Chief's Island in the heart of Moremi Game Reserve, accessible only by light aircraft from Maun (about 1-hour flight).

**Highlights:**

Situated in one of the best wildlife viewing areas in Botswana.

Exclusive game drives and walking safaris led by expert guides.

Large, open-air lounge and dining areas with panoramic views of the Delta.

Pristine wilderness offering sightings of lions, elephants, buffalo, and leopards.

Private plunge pools in each tented suite.

**Spa and Wellness:**

Sanctuary Chief's Camp offers a full-service spa, including massages and wellness treatments, perfect for relaxation after a day of safari.

**Bars:**

The camp features an elegant bar area with a wide selection of drinks, ideal for watching the sunset over the Delta.

**Events and Conferences:**

While primarily a luxury retreat, the camp can cater to small corporate retreats or exclusive events upon request.

**Basic Facilities and Amenities:**

Luxurious safari tents with en-suite bathrooms and private decks.

Air conditioning, mini-bar, and Wi-Fi.

Swimming pool, library, and gift shop.

24-hour security and concierge services.

**Opening and Closing Hours:**
Open year-round, though seasonal variations in rates and availability occur.

**Price:**
Prices range from $900 to $1,500 per night per person, depending on the season.

**Pros:**

Exceptional wildlife experiences, including private game drives and guided walks.

High-end luxury with incredible attention to detail.

Excellent staff and service.

**Cons:**

Expensive, making it inaccessible for budget travelers.

Limited access, as it's only reachable by light aircraft.

**Local Tips:**

Plan to visit during the dry season (May to October) for the best wildlife sightings.

Pack light, as you'll need to take a small plane from Maun to the camp.

2. **Sossusvlei Desert Lodge - Namibia**

Located in the Namib Desert, Sossusvlei Desert Lodge is a stunning desert retreat that offers luxurious accommodations with unparalleled views of the surrounding dunes. It's a perfect getaway for those looking to experience the beauty of the desert in comfort.

**Location (Address & Proximity):**

Situated in the NamibRand Nature Reserve, about 60 km from the Sossusvlei dunes. It is accessible by road from Windhoek (approx. 5-6 hours) or by small aircraft from Windhoek.

**Highlights:**

Surreal views of the Namib Desert's red dunes and mountains.

Excellent stargazing, with the lodge being located in a dark sky reserve.

A wide range of activities including guided desert walks, dune climbing, and scenic drives.

Eco-friendly lodge with solar-powered energy and water conservation measures.

**Spa and Wellness:**

Sossusvlei Desert Lodge has a full-service spa offering massages and wellness treatments. The serene desert environment adds to the peaceful atmosphere of the wellness experiences.

**Bars:**
The lodge offers an elegant bar with indoor and outdoor seating. Guests can enjoy drinks while taking in the spectacular desert sunset.

**Events and Conferences:**

The lodge is ideal for small, intimate events or corporate retreats, with a focus on nature and tranquility rather than large gatherings.

**Basic Facilities and Amenities:**

Spacious stone-and-glass villas with private plunge pools.

Wi-Fi, minibar, and air-conditioning.

Infinity pool and fitness center.

Gourmet dining options, with meals made from fresh, local ingredients.

**Opening and Closing Hours:**

Open year-round, though the best time to visit is during the dry season (April to October).

**Price:**

Prices range from $500 to $1,000 per night, depending on the season and type of accommodation.

**Pros:**

Stunning location with breathtaking desert views.

Excellent for stargazing and nature enthusiasts.

Eco-conscious with minimal environmental impact.

**Cons:**

High price point, making it a more exclusive option.

Remote location with limited access by road.

**Local Tips:**

Visit the iconic Sossusvlei dunes at sunrise or sunset for the best photography opportunities.

Wear sun protection and bring light clothing, as temperatures can soar during the day.

### 3. Desert Rhino Camp - Namibia

Desert Rhino Camp, located in the Damaraland region of Namibia, offers a unique opportunity to track the endangered black rhino in their natural habitat. The camp combines luxury with conservation, providing guests with the chance to contribute to rhino protection efforts.

**Location (Address & Proximity):**

Located in the Palmwag Concession, approximately 350 km from Swakopmund, accessible by road or a short flight from Windhoek or Swakopmund.

**Highlights:**

Rhino tracking with expert guides in the Damaraland region.

Beautiful desert landscapes with dramatic mountains and valleys.

Eco-friendly luxury tents blending into the environment.

Opportunities to spot other desert-adapted wildlife like elephants, giraffes, and springbok.

**Spa and Wellness:**

While the camp does not have a formal spa, guests can unwind with private outdoor massages and enjoy the serenity of the desert surroundings.

**Bars:**
Desert Rhino Camp has a bar area where guests can enjoy a sundowner while watching the sunset over the vast desert landscape.

**Events and Conferences:**

The camp is more focused on small groups and exclusive, nature-focused experiences, making it suitable for private gatherings or intimate corporate retreats.

**Basic Facilities and Amenities:**

Comfortable tented suites with en-suite bathrooms.

Private outdoor shower and plunge pool.

Guided wildlife tracking excursions.

Lounge area with a library and gift shop.

**Opening and Closing Hours:**

Open from March to December, with seasonal variations in pricing.

**Price:**
Prices range from $500 to $800 per night per person, depending on the season.

**Pros:**

Exclusive wildlife experiences, including black rhino tracking.

Eco-friendly luxury with a focus on conservation.

Secluded location offering peace and tranquility.

**Cons:**

Not suitable for those seeking a more traditional lodge experience.

The cost might be too high for budget travelers.

**Local Tips:**

Ensure your camera is ready for stunning wildlife photography, especially during tracking expeditions.

The camp is remote, so be prepared for a more rugged adventure.

### 4. Wolwedans Dune Camp - Namibia

Wolwedans Dune Camp is a unique desert lodge located in the NamibRand Nature Reserve, offering a secluded and immersive desert experience. Guests are treated to panoramic views of the desert, complemented by luxurious tented accommodations.

**Location (Address & Proximity):**

Located in the NamibRand Nature Reserve, about 55 km from the Sossusvlei dunes, it can be reached by light aircraft or via a 4x4 drive from Windhoek (approx. 4 hours).

**Highlights:**

Beautiful and remote location with stunning views of the Namib Desert dunes.

Range of activities, including scenic flights, dune walks, and stargazing.

Focus on sustainable tourism with eco-friendly operations.

Open, spacious tented suites with private decks and plunge pools.

**Spa and Wellness:**

Wolwedans offers wellness treatments in a tranquil desert setting, including massage therapies and relaxation services.

**Bars:**

The camp features an outdoor bar where guests can enjoy refreshing drinks while enjoying the views of the desert dunes.

**Events and Conferences:**

Wolwedans Dune Camp is an excellent choice for private events, offering intimate settings for small weddings, group getaways, or corporate retreats.

**Basic Facilities and Amenities:**

Tented suites with en-suite bathrooms and private plunge pools.

Wi-Fi available in public areas.

Communal dining area and lounge.

Eco-friendly initiatives with solar power and water conservation.

**Opening and Closing Hours:**

Open year-round, although the peak season is from May to October.

**Price:**
Prices range from $400 to $700 per night, depending on the season and accommodation type.

**Pros:**

Stunning desert location with spectacular views.

Great for those looking for an exclusive and eco-conscious experience.

Excellent for stargazing and desert activities.

**Cons:**

Remote location may require a longer journey to reach.

Higher price point, making it inaccessible for some travelers.

**Local Tips:**

Sunrise and sunset are the best times for photography, with the changing colors of the dunes.

Consider a scenic flight to view the full extent of the Namib Desert.

## Booking Tips & Recommendations

### 1. Book in Advance, Especially During Peak Seasons

**Why:** Botswana and Namibia are popular tourist destinations, particularly during the dry season (May to October). Safari camps and desert lodges often have limited availability, especially the high-end or exclusive ones. Booking well in advance increases your chances of securing your preferred accommodation.

**When to Book:** Aim to book at least 6 months in advance, especially for popular camps like **Sanctuary Chief's Camp** or **Sossusvlei Desert Lodge**.

**Pro Tip:** During the off-season (November to April), availability is generally better, and you might find discounts, though some camps may be closed or have limited services.

### 2. Consider the Location and Accessibility

**Why:** Botswana and Namibia's safari camps and desert lodges are often in remote areas, sometimes requiring small aircraft or long drives from major cities.

**Booking Tip:** Ensure that the lodge is accessible via your preferred means of travel, whether it be by road or air. For example, **Sanctuary Chief's Camp** is only reachable by light aircraft from Maun, so plan accordingly.

**Pro Tip:** Some lodges, like **Desert Rhino Camp**, offer a combined flight and road transfer option, so check if there are package deals to make your trip smoother.

### 3. Know the Package Inclusions and Extra Costs

**Why:** Most safari camps and desert lodges offer all-inclusive packages, which typically cover meals, drinks, guided activities, and accommodations. However, certain activities (like private safaris or spa treatments) may incur additional costs.

**Booking Tip:** Review what is included in your booking to avoid surprises. Some lodges offer packages with all meals and activities included, while others may charge separately for special excursions or services.

**Pro Tip:** Check for added value options like complimentary transfers, excursions, or early booking discounts. Sometimes, booking directly with the lodge or camp might provide perks not available through third-party booking sites.

### 4. Understand the Seasonal Pricing

**Why:** Pricing can fluctuate greatly between low and high seasons, with rates typically higher during the dry season (May to October) when wildlife viewing is at its peak.

**Booking Tip:** If you are traveling on a budget, consider visiting during the green season (November to April). This is the wet season, which is less crowded and offers lower rates, but be aware that some lodges might be closed or have reduced activities.

**Pro Tip:** If you are interested in seeing the desert or the wildlife in the Okavango Delta at their most vibrant, the dry season is ideal, but if you're looking for a more peaceful experience with fewer tourists, the green season can be a hidden gem.

### 5. Check the Lodge's Commitment to Sustainability

**Why:** Many safari camps and desert lodges in Botswana and Namibia are eco-friendly and committed to sustainable tourism. This includes using solar energy, water conservation efforts, and responsible wildlife interaction.

**Booking Tip:** Look for properties that are part of eco-tourism initiatives or conservation efforts, such as **Sossusvlei Desert Lodge** in the NamibRand Nature Reserve or **Desert Rhino Camp** in Damaraland.

**Pro Tip:** Ask about the lodge's sustainability practices before booking, such as how they support wildlife conservation or minimize their environmental footprint. This ensures your stay aligns with eco-conscious travel goals.

### 6. Verify the Lodge's Activities and Facilities

**Why:** Each safari camp and desert lodge offers a unique set of activities, such as guided game drives, nature walks, and cultural experiences. Knowing what's available will help you select the property that best matches your interests.

**Booking Tip:** Confirm the activities included in the package, like wildlife tracking, stargazing, or scenic drives. For example, **Sossusvlei Desert Lodge** offers excellent stargazing, while **Sanctuary Chief's Camp** provides game drives in the Okavango Delta.

**Pro Tip:** Some lodges offer specialized experiences, such as private guided safaris or photography tours. If these experiences are important to you, inquire about customization options when booking.

### 7. Ask About Special Offers and Packages

**Why:** Many safari camps and desert lodges offer special promotions, such as honeymoon packages, family discounts, or group rates. These can make your trip more affordable and enjoyable.

**Booking Tip:** Inquire about discounts for longer stays (e.g., stay for 5 nights, pay for 4) or seasonal promotions, as many camps offer such packages during off-peak times.

**Pro Tip:** Many lodges and camps offer exclusive experiences or packages for special occasions (weddings, birthdays, anniversaries), including private dinners, personalized safaris, and spa treatments.

### 8. Consider Travel Insurance

**Why:** Traveling to remote areas means being prepared for unexpected events, from delayed flights to medical emergencies or changes in travel plans.

**Booking Tip:** It's wise to purchase comprehensive travel insurance that covers trip cancellations, lost luggage, and medical emergencies. Some safari camps may have policies in place for cancellations or delays, but it's always best to be prepared.

**Pro Tip:** Ensure that your travel insurance covers emergency evacuation in case of a medical situation while in a remote area.

### 9. Check Reviews and Testimonials

**Why:** While all lodges and camps boast about their offerings, checking online reviews and testimonials from past guests can give you an honest sense of the quality of the experience, the service, and the accommodations.

**Booking Tip:** Websites like TripAdvisor, Google Reviews, and safari-specific review sites can help you gauge customer satisfaction and see firsthand accounts of experiences.

**Pro Tip:** Look for reviews that mention specific details, like the quality of the food, wildlife sightings, and the knowledge of the guides. This will help you avoid surprises and make a more informed choice.

## 10. Confirm the Lodge's Covid-19 Protocols (if applicable)

**Why:** Due to the global pandemic, many accommodations have updated their policies regarding health and safety, particularly in remote areas where healthcare access may be limited.

**Booking Tip:** Before booking, verify the lodge's Covid-19 protocols, including cleaning procedures, social distancing practices, and any health requirements.

**Pro Tip:** Many lodges offer flexible booking policies, such as free cancellations or rebooking options in case of travel restrictions.

# Chapter 4: Top Attractions in Botswana

## Chobe National Park & Wildlife Safari

Chobe National Park is one of Botswana's premier wildlife destinations, renowned for its vast landscapes, diverse ecosystems, and an abundance of wildlife. Situated in the northern part of the country, it is famous for its large elephant population, which is the largest in the world. The park is a haven for safaris and a must-see destination for wildlife enthusiasts.

**Location**

Chobe National Park is located in the northeastern region of Botswana, near the town of Kasane. It borders the Chobe River, which provides water for many species, and is close to the borders of Namibia, Zimbabwe, and Zambia, making it easily accessible from several international gateways.

**History**

Chobe National Park was established in 1968, making it Botswana's first national park. It was created to protect the wildlife in the region, particularly the elephants that migrated across the Chobe River. Over the years, the park has expanded to cover 11,700 square kilometers of wilderness, showcasing a variety of habitats including floodplains, savannah, woodlands, and riverine ecosystems.

## Opening and Closing Hours

Chobe National Park is open year-round, and the best time to visit depends on your preference for wildlife viewing:

**Daytime**: The park is generally accessible during daylight hours for game drives and safari activities.

**Safari Activities**: Most game drives and boat tours are organized early in the morning and in the late afternoon to maximize wildlife viewing.

## Top Things to Do

**Safari Game Drives**: A top activity, these guided excursions take visitors into the park's interior where they can spot lions, leopards, buffalo, zebras, and an array of bird species. Chobe is particularly known for its large herds of elephants.

**Boat Cruises on the Chobe River**: These provide unique views of wildlife, especially elephants and hippos, as they congregate along the riverbanks. The river is a crucial water source for many animals in the dry season.

**Bird Watching**: Chobe is a paradise for bird watchers with over 450 bird species. The park offers diverse habitats, from wetlands to forested areas, attracting birds like the African fish eagle and the white-crowned lapwing.

**Photographic Safaris**: With its breathtaking landscapes and rich wildlife, Chobe is a photographer's dream. Special photo safaris are offered for capturing the best wildlife moments.

**Fishing**: The Chobe River offers great opportunities for catch-and-release fishing, with species such as tigerfish and bream.

## Practical Information

**Getting There**: The easiest way to reach Chobe is via Kasane, which has an international airport with flights from Johannesburg, Maun, and Victoria Falls. Alternatively, travelers can drive to the park from neighboring countries.

**Accommodation**: The park has a variety of accommodation options ranging from luxury lodges to basic campsites. Options such as Chobe Game Lodge and the Chobe Safari Lodge offer all-inclusive packages with safari activities.

**Safety**: Visitors are advised to follow park regulations, especially when encountering wildlife. Safari guides are well-trained and offer safe experiences.

**Tips for Visiting**

**Best Time to Visit**: The dry season (May to October) is ideal for wildlife viewing, especially elephants as they gather along the river.

**What to Pack**: Lightweight clothing, binoculars, a good camera, and sunscreen are essential. Bring a hat and mosquito repellent.

**Guides**: Hiring a knowledgeable guide will enrich your safari experience, as they provide valuable insights into animal behavior and the park's ecosystems.

## Okavango Delta: Mokoro Rides & Game Viewing

The Okavango Delta is one of the most unique inland deltas in the world and a UNESCO World Heritage Site. This vast wetland oasis, formed by seasonal flooding, supports an incredibly diverse range of wildlife and plant life. Visitors come from all over the world to explore its waterways by mokoro (traditional dugout canoe), engage in thrilling game drives, and experience a pristine wilderness like no other.

## Location

The Okavango Delta is located in the northwest of Botswana, covering an area of approximately 15,000 square kilometers. It is situated in the Kalahari Desert basin, where the Okavango River spreads out, forming an intricate network of channels, lagoons, and islands.

## History

The Okavango Delta has formed over millennia due to the fluctuating water levels of the Okavango River. It was declared a UNESCO World Heritage Site in 2014 due to its exceptional natural beauty, biodiversity, and the ecological significance of the area. The delta is home to the indigenous San people, and it continues to support a wide variety of wildlife and vegetation.

## Opening and Closing Hours

The Okavango Delta is open year-round. However, activities like mokoro rides and game drives are best undertaken during the dry season (May to October), when wildlife congregates near water sources. The flood season (April to August) transforms the landscape into a watery paradise, ideal for bird watching and aquatic life observation.

## Top Things to Do

**Mokoro Rides**: The highlight of a visit to the Okavango Delta is a mokoro ride. These traditional canoes, guided by local polers, navigate the narrow channels of the delta, offering a peaceful and intimate wildlife experience. It's an excellent way to view hippos, crocodiles, and water birds up close.

**Game Drives**: Visitors can explore the delta's floodplains and islands on safari game drives, where they can see the "Big Five" (lion, leopard, elephant, buffalo, and rhino) along with a variety of antelope, zebra, and wildebeest.

**Walking Safaris**: Accompanied by expert guides, walking safaris allow tourists to explore the wilderness on foot, learning about the ecology and tracking wildlife.

**Bird Watching**: The Okavango Delta is a birdwatcher's paradise, with more than 400 species, including pelicans, herons, and rare birds like the Wattled Crane.

**Fishing**: Fishing is a popular activity in certain areas of the delta, where anglers can catch species like tigerfish and tilapia.

## Practical Information

**Getting There**: The Okavango Delta is best accessed from Maun, which is serviced by regular flights from major cities like Johannesburg and Gaborone. From Maun, visitors take light aircraft flights or chartered helicopters to smaller airstrips near the delta.

**Accommodation**: The delta is home to a range of accommodations, from luxurious lodges like Sanctuary Chief's Camp to more rustic and eco-friendly campsites. Many lodges offer all-inclusive packages with mokoro rides, game drives, and guided walks.

**Health and Safety**: Visitors should ensure they are up-to-date on vaccinations (especially for malaria) and consult with a health professional before traveling. It is also important to follow the park rules and listen to the guides for safety, especially when interacting with wildlife.

## Tips for Visiting

**Best Time to Visit**: The dry season (May to October) offers the best wildlife sightings and ideal conditions for mokoro rides. However, the flooding season (April to August) provides a different kind of beauty with water activities.

**What to Pack**: Light clothing, binoculars, a camera, a wide-brimmed hat, sunscreen, and insect repellent. Don't forget to pack a flashlight and a good pair of walking shoes for safaris.

**Local Etiquette**: Respect the local culture, particularly the indigenous communities in the area. When on mokoro rides or safaris, keep noise to a minimum to avoid disturbing wildlife.

# Moremi Game Reserve & Savuti Wildlife

Moremi Game Reserve is one of Botswana's most renowned protected areas, located in the eastern part of the Okavango Delta. It is celebrated for its diverse wildlife, lush vegetation, and variety of ecosystems, including forests, floodplains, and marshes. The reserve provides one of the best safari experiences in Africa, with high chances of spotting rare and endangered species. Savuti, located within the reserve, is famous for its dramatic wildlife encounters, particularly its large predator populations.

**Location**

Moremi Game Reserve lies in the northeastern part of Botswana, covering over 5,000 square kilometers. It is situated on the eastern side of the Okavango Delta, bordered by the Khwai River in the north and the Savuti Channel in the west. Savuti is a particular region within Moremi, known for its unique wildlife and topography.

**History**

Moremi Game Reserve was established in 1963 to protect the rich biodiversity of the Okavango Delta. The reserve was named after the wife of the chief of the BaTawana people, who was instrumental in its creation. Savuti, part of the reserve, has been a center for wildlife observation, especially for predator sightings.

## Opening and Closing Hours

**Opening Hours**: The reserve is open year-round, though it is best to visit during the dry season (May to October) for optimal wildlife viewing. Activities such as game drives and guided walking safaris are typically conducted from early morning to late afternoon.

**Safari Activities**: Guided game drives, walking safaris, and boat cruises operate during the day, with some lodges offering night drives for wildlife sightings under the stars.

## Top Things to Do

**Game Drives**: Moremi offers fantastic game drive opportunities. Wildlife sightings here include the "Big Five" (lions, leopards, elephants, buffalo, and rhino) as well as cheetahs, wild dogs, and hippos.

**Savuti Wildlife Viewing**: Known for its dramatic wildlife, Savuti is famous for predator sightings, especially lions and cheetahs. The seasonal variation in the water levels of the Savuti Channel creates a unique setting for observing large concentrations of animals.

**Bird Watching**: With over 400 bird species, Moremi is a birdwatcher's haven, including species like the African fish eagle and the endangered wattled crane.

**Walking Safaris**: These allow visitors to experience the landscape from a different perspective, offering close encounters with nature and the opportunity to learn about the reserve's ecosystems from expert guides.

## Practical Information

**Getting There**: Moremi can be accessed via airstrips near the reserve, with flights from Maun and other major cities. Private safari companies often offer chartered flights to the region. There are also 4x4 roads to the reserve for self-drive safaris.

**Accommodation**: Moremi and Savuti offer various accommodations, including luxury lodges, tented camps, and camping sites. Lodges such as Xakanaxa, Khwai River Lodge, and Savuti Safari Lodge provide excellent safari experiences.

**Tips for Visiting**

**Best Time to Visit**: The dry season (May to October) is ideal for wildlife viewing as animals gather around water sources. However, visiting during the wet season (November to April) offers birdwatching opportunities and lush landscapes.

**What to Pack**: Bring neutral-colored clothing, a good camera, binoculars, sunscreen, insect repellent, and a hat. Also, pack light, breathable clothing for hot weather and warm layers for early morning safaris.

**Guides**: Local guides provide valuable insights into wildlife behavior, animal tracking, and the reserve's ecosystems, enriching the experience.

## Makgadikgadi Pans & Kubu Island

The Makgadikgadi Pans, part of the Kalahari Desert, are one of the largest salt pans in the world, offering a surreal and starkly beautiful landscape. The vast, dry expanses of the pans are home to a unique ecosystem, including wildlife and ancient salt deposits. Kubu Island, situated in the middle of the pans, is an iconic site known for its Baobab trees and archaeological significance. This area offers a unique contrast to the lush landscapes of Botswana's more traditional wildlife reserves.

## Location

The Makgadikgadi Pans are located in the northern part of Botswana, within the Kalahari Desert. Kubu Island lies within the Makgadikgadi Pans and is one of the most popular destinations in the area, accessible via 4x4 vehicles.

## History

The Makgadikgadi Pans were once part of an ancient lake, which covered much of Botswana thousands of years ago. Over time, the lake dried up, leaving behind these vast salt pans. Kubu Island holds cultural and historical significance, with evidence of ancient human activity, including stone tools and rock engravings.

## Opening and Closing Hours

**Opening Hours**: The Makgadikgadi Pans and Kubu Island are accessible year-round, but it is best to visit during the dry season (May to October) when the roads are passable and the area's wildlife is easier to spot.

**Best Time to Visit**: The wet season (November to April) can be challenging for access but provides the opportunity to witness seasonal migratory species, particularly wildebeest and zebra.

## Top Things to Do

**Explore Kubu Island**: Visit this historic island with its ancient Baobab trees and remnants of past human settlements. It is an excellent spot for photography, stargazing, and wildlife watching.

**Game Viewing**: While the Makgadikgadi Pans are arid, the surrounding areas are home to a variety of wildlife, including meerkats, springbok, and the occasional wildebeest or zebra. The migration of zebra and wildebeest is an incredible spectacle in the wet season.

**Quad Biking**: Explore the salt pans on a quad bike to experience the vast emptiness and unique landscape up close.

**Bird Watching**: The pans are home to a number of bird species, particularly during the wet season, when migratory birds arrive to take advantage of the temporary water sources.

**Practical Information**

**Getting There**: The Makgadikgadi Pans and Kubu Island can be accessed by 4x4 vehicles, which are available for hire from Maun. Charter flights also operate to nearby airstrips.

**Accommodation**: There are limited options for staying near the pans, with small lodges and campsites available. Kubu Island is often explored on day trips, and camping is available at designated sites.

**Tips for Visiting**

**What to Pack**: Due to the extreme heat, pack lightweight clothing, sunscreen, plenty of water, and sturdy footwear for walking in the pans. Don't forget a camera for the stunning landscapes.

**Be Prepared for Isolation**: The Makgadikgadi Pans are remote, and visitors should be prepared for a lack of amenities. It's recommended to travel with a guide and ensure you have enough fuel, food, and water.

## Central Kalahari Game Reserve & Deception Valley

The Central Kalahari Game Reserve is one of the largest conservation areas in the world, covering about 52,000 square kilometers. The reserve is known for its stark beauty and the variety of wildlife that thrives in the arid Kalahari Desert.

Deception Valley, located within the reserve, is a famous area known for its wildlife sightings, especially during the rainy season when it transforms into a lush paradise.

## Location

The Central Kalahari Game Reserve is situated in the heart of Botswana, covering the central and southern regions of the Kalahari Desert. Deception Valley is located in the northeastern section of the reserve and is particularly popular for game viewing.

## History

The reserve was established in 1961 to protect the wildlife of the Kalahari region, including the San people's ancestral lands. It was one of the last regions in southern Africa to be protected, and it remains one of the most remote and untouched wildlife areas in Botswana.

## Opening and Closing Hours

**Opening Hours**: The reserve is open year-round. However, the best time to visit is during the wet season (November to March) when wildlife is most concentrated around the waterholes and predators are more active.

**Safari Activities**: Game drives, walking safaris, and camping are the main activities, typically starting early in the morning and ending at sunset.

## Top Things to Do

**Game Drives in Deception Valley**: Known for its excellent predator sightings, including lions, cheetahs, and hyenas, Deception Valley is a top destination for those seeking an authentic safari experience.

**Wildlife Watching**: The Kalahari is home to various wildlife, including springbok, gemsbok, jackals, and the elusive brown hyena. During the rainy season, the valley comes alive with wildebeest and zebra migrations.

**Walking Safaris**: Led by local guides, walking safaris allow visitors to track wildlife on foot and gain deeper insights into the Kalahari ecosystem.

## Practical Information

**Getting There**: The reserve can be reached by air from Maun to nearby airstrips or by 4x4 vehicles. Driving within the reserve requires a permit, and self-drive visitors need to be well-prepared for remote conditions.

**Accommodation**: Camping is the most common form of accommodation within the reserve, with a few small lodges available for those seeking more comfort.

## Tips for Visiting

**Best Time to Visit**: The wet season (November to March) is ideal for wildlife migrations, while the dry season (April to October) offers better conditions for traveling across the park.

**What to Pack**: Prepare for extreme conditions by packing lightweight, neutral-colored clothing, sun protection, and enough food and water for long drives. The Kalahari can be very hot, so a wide-brimmed hat and sunglasses are essential.

# Chapter 5: Top Attractions in Namibia
## Etosha National Park & The Big Five

Etosha National Park is one of Namibia's premier wildlife destinations, recognized worldwide for its vast salt pans, abundant wildlife, and stunning landscapes. Covering 22,270 square kilometers, Etosha is a sanctuary for a wide variety of animals, including the famed "Big Five" — lions, leopards, elephants, buffalo, and rhinoceros. It's also home to over 300 bird species, making it a fantastic destination for both wildlife enthusiasts and bird watchers.

### Location

Etosha National Park is located in the northern part of Namibia, primarily in the Kunene Region. It is approximately 400 kilometers from the capital city, Windhoek, and can be accessed via the town of Tsumeb, which is close to the park's southern entrance.

### History

The park was established in 1907 and is one of Africa's oldest and largest wildlife reserves. Its centerpiece is the vast Etosha Pan, a large salt flat that is often dry, but floods during the rainy season, creating a unique ecosystem. The name

"Etosha" comes from the Ovambo word "Etosha," meaning "great white place," which refers to the immense salt pans that dominate the park's landscape.

## Opening and Closing Hours

**Opening Hours**: Etosha National Park is open year-round. However, some areas are only accessible during daylight hours, typically from sunrise to sunset.

**Best Time to Visit**: The dry season (May to October) is the most popular for wildlife viewing, as animals concentrate around waterholes. During the wet season (November to April), the park becomes lush, and birdlife flourishes, though wildlife may be harder to spot.

## Top Things to Do

**Game Drives**: Etosha offers exceptional game viewing opportunities, especially around the park's waterholes, where animals gather to drink. Visitors can expect to see large herds of elephants, giraffes, zebras, wildebeest, and impalas. The "Big Five" — lions, elephants, rhinos, buffalo, and leopards — can all be found in the park, with lions and elephants being the most frequently spotted.

**Wildlife Viewing at Waterholes**: The park is known for its numerous waterholes, such as Okaukuejo and Halali, where visitors can view a variety of wildlife, including predators, during the early morning or late afternoon.

**Bird Watching**: With over 300 species of birds, Etosha is a paradise for bird watchers. Species such as the flamingo, secretary bird, and several species of vultures, storks, and eagles are commonly seen.

**Night Game Drives**: Some of the park's lodges offer night safari drives, where you can observe nocturnal animals like leopards, hyenas, and owls.

**Guided Walks**: There are several guided walks available where tourists can learn about the park's flora and fauna, including the medicinal uses of indigenous plants.

## Practical Information

**Getting There**: Etosha National Park is accessible by car or air. The nearest major town to the park is Tsumeb, and it is about a 4-5 hour drive from Windhoek. You can also reach the park via scheduled flights to the park's airstrips.

**Accommodation**: The park offers various accommodation options ranging from campsites to luxury lodges. Okaukuejo, Halali, and Namutoni are the main lodges within the park, offering excellent facilities and wildlife viewing opportunities.

**Tips for Visiting**

**Best Time to Visit**: The dry season (May to October) is the best time for wildlife viewing, as animals are drawn to the waterholes. However, the wet season (November to April) offers a lush green landscape and excellent birdwatching.

**What to Pack**: Pack neutral-colored clothing for safaris, a wide-brimmed hat, sunscreen, binoculars, a camera with a zoom lens, and insect repellent.

**Guides**: Hiring a local guide will greatly enhance your experience, providing insights into animal behavior and the park's ecosystems.

## Sossusvlei & Deadvlei: Namibia's Iconic Dunes

Sossusvlei and Deadvlei are among Namibia's most iconic natural landscapes, offering some of the most striking desert views in the world. Located in the heart of the Namib Desert, these two areas are famous for their towering red dunes, surreal salt pans, and ancient dead trees. Sossusvlei, meaning "dead-end marsh,"

is a salt and clay pan surrounded by some of the tallest dunes on the planet, while Deadvlei features a striking contrast of white clay and blackened, ancient camel thorn trees. These landscapes are a must-see for visitors to Namibia.

## Location

Sossusvlei and Deadvlei are situated in the southern part of the Namib Desert, within the Namib-Naukluft National Park. The nearest major town is Sesriem, which is about 60 kilometers from the entrance to the park. The dunes are located along the Tsauchab River, although the river is dry for much of the year.

## History

The Namib Desert is one of the oldest deserts in the world, with some areas dating back as far as 55 million years. The iconic dunes of Sossusvlei and Deadvlei were formed by the shifting sands and wind patterns over thousands of years, creating vast landscapes of sand dunes and clay pans. The dead trees in Deadvlei are believed to be between 600 and 900 years old, having died when the Tsauchab River shifted course.

## Opening and Closing Hours

**Opening Hours**: Sossusvlei and Deadvlei are generally open from sunrise to sunset. The park gates open early in the morning, and visitors are encouraged to arrive at sunrise to capture the best light and to avoid the heat of midday.

**Best Time to Visit**: The best time to visit is during the cooler months (May to October) when temperatures are more moderate. The dunes are most photogenic at sunrise and sunset when the light creates long shadows and highlights the rich red color of the sand.

## Top Things to Do

**Climb the Dunes**: The towering dunes of Sossusvlei, including the famous Dune 45, are a highlight of any visit. Visitors can hike up the dunes to enjoy panoramic views of the surrounding desert. The sunrise or sunset hike offers the best light for photography.

**Explore Deadvlei**: The striking white clay pan of Deadvlei, surrounded by red dunes and dotted with dead camel thorn trees, creates an eerie, otherworldly landscape. This area is perfect for photography and offers a contrast to the vibrant colors of the dunes.

**Visit Sossusvlei**: The salt and clay pan of Sossusvlei is an iconic destination. From here, visitors can view the surrounding dunes and take in the incredible scale and beauty of the landscape.

**Scenic Flights**: Take a scenic flight over the dunes to see the vastness of the desert and gain a unique perspective of the landscape. These flights often provide views of the Skeleton Coast and the unique topography of the desert.

**Sandboarding and Quad Biking**: For those looking for adventure, sandboarding and quad biking are popular activities in the dunes, offering a thrilling way to experience the desert.

## Practical Information

**Getting There**: The main access point to Sossusvlei and Deadvlei is via Sesriem, which can be reached by car from Windhoek or Swakopmund. It is a 5-hour drive from Windhoek to Sesriem. There are also chartered flights available to the nearby airstrips.

**Accommodation**: Accommodation options range from campsites to luxury lodges near Sesriem, such as Sossusvlei Desert Lodge and Desert Camp. The accommodation near the park gates offers easy access to the dunes at sunrise.

## Tips for Visiting

**Best Time to Visit**: Visit early in the morning or late in the afternoon to avoid the midday heat and to capture the dunes in their most photogenic light.

**What to Pack**: Bring light clothing for the day and warm clothing for the early mornings and evenings. Sunscreen, a hat, water, and sturdy shoes for dune climbing are also essential.

**Guides**: Consider hiring a local guide who can provide insights into the desert's ecosystem, geology, and history.

# Skeleton Coast & Shipwreck Adventures

The Skeleton Coast is one of Namibia's most desolate and fascinating regions, characterized by its rugged coastline, arid landscape, and eerie remnants of shipwrecks. The coast earned its name due to the numerous ships that have been stranded or wrecked along its shores due to the dense fog, dangerous currents, and rocky coastline. The area is part of the larger Skeleton Coast National Park, which spans over 16,000 square kilometers and offers an otherworldly experience with its stark beauty, wildlife, and historical intrigue.

**Location**

The Skeleton Coast is located in the northwestern part of Namibia, stretching along the Atlantic Ocean from the Ugab River to the Angolan border. It is one of the most remote areas of Namibia, accessible mainly by 4x4 vehicles or light aircraft, with access through various airstrips in the region.

**History**

The Skeleton Coast has a long history of shipwrecks, many of which occurred during the 19th and early 20th centuries due to the treacherous waters. The coast's name comes from both the remains of shipwrecks and the skeletal remains of whales that were once abundant in the area. The region also has historical significance as it was home to indigenous peoples like the Himba, who adapted to the harsh conditions of the desert.

## Opening and Closing Hours

**Opening Hours**: The Skeleton Coast is open year-round, though access to the park is limited due to its remote nature and conservation efforts. Visitors need to obtain permits to visit the park, and the best way to explore it is by guided tour.

**Best Time to Visit**: The cooler months between May and October are the best for visiting, as the weather is more moderate and the chances of fog are lower. The summer months (November to April) are hotter, and fog can obscure visibility along the coast.

## Top Things to Do

**Shipwreck Viewing**: The Skeleton Coast is famous for its haunting shipwrecks, which dot the shoreline. One of the most famous is the wreck of the *Eduard Bohlen*, which is partially buried in the sand. You can also see the wrecks of the *Dunedin Star* and *Shannon* along with other ghostly remains of vessels that perished in the treacherous waters.

**Wildlife Viewing**: Despite its harsh climate, the Skeleton Coast is home to diverse wildlife. Visitors can spot desert-adapted elephants, lions, seals, and a variety of bird species. The Cape fur seal colonies at Cape Cross are a must-see.

**Scenic Flights**: Aerial views of the Skeleton Coast provide a unique perspective of the region's desolation and beauty. Scenic flights also offer the chance to see shipwrecks and coastal wildlife from the sky.

**Exploring the Desolate Landscape**: The stark, sandy dunes and rocky shores of the Skeleton Coast are mesmerizing to explore. Guided 4x4 tours allow visitors to travel deeper into the park and learn about the local ecosystems and history.

## Practical Information

**Getting There**: The Skeleton Coast can be accessed by light aircraft from Swakopmund or other nearby towns. There are several airstrips within the park. You can also reach the coast by 4x4 vehicles, but the terrain can be challenging, so experienced drivers and guided tours are recommended.

**Accommodation**: There are a limited number of luxury lodges and camps that offer guided tours of the Skeleton Coast, including accommodations such as the Skeleton Coast Camp. These offer remote, comfortable stays in this wilderness region.

**Tips for Visiting**

**Guided Tours**: Due to the remote and rugged nature of the coast, it's advisable to visit with a guide who knows the terrain and can provide insight into the shipwrecks and local wildlife.

**Permits**: A permit is required to visit the Skeleton Coast National Park, and these can be obtained through the Namibia Wildlife Resorts or guided tour operators.

**What to Pack**: Pack light clothing for daytime, warm layers for the cooler evenings, sunscreen, a hat, and plenty of water.

## Fish River Canyon: Africa's Grand Canyon

Fish River Canyon, located in southern Namibia, is one of the largest and most impressive canyons in the world. Spanning over 160 kilometers in length, up to 27 kilometers in width, and up to 550 meters deep, it is often referred to as "Africa's Grand Canyon." The canyon was formed around 500 million years ago and offers visitors breathtaking views and a range of outdoor activities.

## Location

Fish River Canyon is located in the southern part of Namibia, near the border with South Africa. It lies about 700 kilometers south of Windhoek, the capital city, and is easily accessible by road. The canyon is part of the Fish River Canyon Park, which is situated in the Namibian semi-desert region.

## History

The canyon was formed by a combination of geological processes, including tectonic activity and erosion, which have shaped the dramatic landscape seen today. The Fish River itself once carved its way through the canyon, although the river no longer flows through it year-round. The canyon has significant archaeological importance, with evidence of ancient human settlements and rock engravings found in the area.

## Opening and Closing Hours

**Opening Hours**: Fish River Canyon is open to visitors throughout the year. The best times for viewing the canyon are during the early morning or late afternoon, when the light creates stunning contrasts across the rock formations.

**Best Time to Visit**: The cooler months between May and October are ideal for visiting, as the temperatures are more moderate. The summer months can be very hot, making it challenging to explore the canyon comfortably.

## Top Things to Do

**Canyon Viewing**: The primary attraction at Fish River Canyon is simply taking in the awe-inspiring views from various viewpoints around the canyon's rim. The main viewpoint is at the southern end of the canyon, providing a sweeping vista of the landscape.

**Hiking**: The Fish River Canyon offers some incredible hiking opportunities, including the Fish River Canyon Trail, a 5-day trek that takes you from the rim to the bottom of the canyon. It's a strenuous hike, so it's recommended for experienced trekkers.

**Scenic Flights**: For a different perspective of the canyon, visitors can take scenic flights over the canyon and surrounding areas, offering a bird's eye view of the scale and beauty of the canyon.

**Camping**: There are several campsites located around the canyon, offering a chance to camp under the stars and experience the desert landscape up close.

## Practical Information

**Getting There**: The Fish River Canyon is accessible by road from Windhoek or from the town of Keetmanshoop. It is a popular stop along Namibia's southern tourist route.

**Accommodation**: There are a variety of accommodations near the canyon, including campsites, lodges, and guesthouses. The Canyon Lodge offers a luxurious experience with spectacular views of the canyon.

## Tips for Visiting

**Best Time to Visit**: The best time to visit is during the dry season, from May to October, when temperatures are more comfortable. The canyon is especially stunning at sunrise and sunset.

**What to Pack**: Bring sturdy hiking shoes, sunscreen, plenty of water, and warm layers for the evenings. A good camera is essential to capture the magnificent landscapes.

# Damaraland & Twyfelfontein Rock Engravings

Damaraland is a region in northwestern Namibia known for its striking landscapes, wildlife, and archaeological sites. It is home to some of the country's most ancient rock art, including the famous Twyfelfontein Rock Engravings, which are one of the largest concentrations of petroglyphs (rock carvings) in Africa. The area is also known for its desert-adapted wildlife, such as elephants, lions, and rhinos.

## Location

Damaraland is located in the northwestern part of Namibia, and it covers a vast area of rugged terrain, including mountains, valleys, and plains. Twyfelfontein, the site of the rock engravings, is situated within Damaraland, about 400 kilometers from Windhoek.

## History

Damaraland has been inhabited by various groups for thousands of years. The region is rich in archaeological history, particularly in the form of rock art. Twyfelfontein was used by ancient hunter-gatherers, and its rock engravings date back over 6,000 years. The engravings depict various animals, including elephants, giraffes, and lions, as well as abstract symbols.

## Opening and Closing Hours

**Opening Hours**: Twyfelfontein is open year-round, with the best time to visit being during the dry season, from May to October.

**Best Time to Visit**: The cooler months are ideal for visiting Damaraland and Twyfelfontein, as the temperatures can be extremely hot in the summer.

## Top Things to Do

**Explore Twyfelfontein**: The main attraction in Damaraland is the Twyfelfontein Rock Engravings. Visitors can take guided tours to view the carvings, which provide insight into the lives of the ancient inhabitants of the region.

**Wildlife Viewing**: Damaraland is home to desert-adapted elephants, lions, and rhinos. The area is also known for its diverse birdlife, including eagles and vultures.

**Visit Burnt Mountain and Organ Pipes**: Damaraland offers stunning geological formations, including the Burnt Mountain, which features layers of rock that appear to have been set on fire, and the Organ Pipes, a collection of basalt columns.

## Practical Information

**Getting There**: Damaraland is accessible by road from Windhoek or Swakopmund. Twyfelfontein can be reached by a gravel road.

**Accommodation**: There are several accommodations in the area, including campsites and lodges such as Twyfelfontein Country Lodge, which provides a comfortable base for exploring the region.

## Tips for Visiting

**Guided Tours**: Hiring a local guide at Twyfelfontein is recommended to understand the significance of the rock engravings and learn about the history of the area.

**What to Pack**: Wear sturdy hiking shoes, a hat, sunscreen, and bring plenty of water. A camera is essential to capture the stunning landscapes and rock engravings.

# Chapter 6: Outdoor Activities & Adventure

## Safari Experiences: Game Drives & Walking Safaris

Botswana and Namibia are both renowned for their extraordinary outdoor activities, where visitors can experience thrilling adventures amidst their rich, diverse landscapes. Two of the most popular activities that provide unforgettable memories are safari experiences, including game drives and walking safaris, and hot air balloon rides over the desert. These activities offer unique and immersive ways to explore the wild and natural beauty of these countries.

**Safari Experiences: Game Drives & Walking Safaris**

**1. Game Drives in Botswana:** Botswana is one of Africa's premier safari destinations, known for its vast wildlife-rich areas such as the Okavango Delta, Chobe National Park, and Makgadikgadi Pans. The country is famous for offering some of the most exceptional game-viewing experiences in the world. Game drives are an integral part of any safari, where visitors embark on guided tours in open 4x4 vehicles to explore the wilderness.

**What to Expect:**

**Wildlife Sightings:** Game drives provide a great opportunity to observe big game such as elephants, lions, leopards, rhinos, and buffalo, as well as a variety of antelope, zebras, and giraffes. Botswana is renowned for its elephant populations, particularly in Chobe National Park, where visitors can encounter large herds, often near the Chobe River.

**Scenic Views:** Game drives take you across diverse terrains, from lush wetlands to arid savannahs. Travelers can witness Botswana's diverse ecosystems and unique landscapes while spotting wildlife along the way.

**Guides and Expertise:** Professional guides lead game drives, providing guests with detailed information on the animals, plant life, and the ecology of the region. Their expert knowledge increases the chances of spotting elusive animals like leopards or wild dogs.

**2. Walking Safaris in Botswana:** For a more immersive and intimate experience, **walking safaris** offer a chance to explore the wilderness on foot. These safaris are led by skilled and experienced guides who are trained to track animals and interpret the subtle signs of nature.

**What to Expect:**

**Close Encounters with Nature:** Walking safaris allow visitors to get up close to nature, observing animals and plants in a way that's not possible from a vehicle. While walking through the bush, guides point out tracks, scat, and other signs of wildlife activity that are easy to miss from a car.

**Small-Group, Personal Experience:** Walking safaris are often done in small groups, giving guests a more personalized adventure. The experience is often quieter and more peaceful than game drives, offering opportunities for photography, birdwatching, and deeper engagement with the environment.

**Safety and Knowledge:** While walking safaris bring you closer to wildlife, they are always conducted with an emphasis on safety. Guides are adept at ensuring the safety of the group while providing informative talks on animal behavior, ecosystems, and survival skills.

**3. Best Locations for Safari Experiences in Botswana:**

**Okavango Delta:** A UNESCO World Heritage site, the Okavango Delta is a paradise for game viewing and birdwatching. It offers both water-based safaris (via mokoro boats) and land-based safari experiences.

**Chobe National Park:** Known for its large elephant population, it's one of the best places in Africa to see these majestic creatures. Chobe is also home to abundant predators like lions, leopards, and cheetahs.

**Makgadikgadi Pans:** A vast salt pan, ideal for adventurous travelers seeking a more remote, surreal experience with unique wildlife sightings, especially during the green season when migrating zebras and wildebeest arrive.

## Hot Air Balloon Rides Over the Desert:

Namibia is home to the Namib Desert, one of the most awe-inspiring and ancient deserts in the world. Hot air balloon rides over the desert provide a unique perspective of the landscape, offering a serene and breathtaking experience for those visiting the country on vacation.

**1. Hot Air Balloon Experience in Namibia:** In Namibia, **Sossusvlei**, located in the heart of the Namib Desert, is a prime location for hot air balloon rides. This area features iconic **red sand dunes**, some of the highest in the world, which provide the perfect backdrop for an unforgettable balloon adventure.

**What to Expect:**

**Aerial Views of the Desert:** As the hot air balloon ascends, passengers are treated to panoramic views of the vast, undulating sand dunes, which stretch for miles. The early morning light creates stunning contrasts and shades, making the desert landscape even more magical.

**Majestic Sunrise:** The hot air balloon ride typically begins at sunrise, when the desert is bathed in a soft, golden glow. The beauty of the desert during this time is nothing short of breathtaking, as the rising sun casts shadows and illuminates the dunes, giving the landscape an ethereal quality.

**Serenity and Tranquility:** The hot air balloon ride is incredibly peaceful, with the only sounds being the occasional burst of the burner and the natural quiet of the desert. It offers a stark contrast to the more adrenaline-pumping activities, providing a calming, reflective experience.

**2. Best Time to Go:**

The best time to experience hot air balloon rides in Namibia is during the **dry season** (from April to October). During these months, the weather is cooler, with clear skies and mild winds, which are ideal for balloon flights.

**3. What You'll See:**

**Desert Landscapes:** From the sky, visitors get a bird's-eye view of the vast stretches of red dunes, unique rock formations, dry riverbeds, and salt pans. This area is so remote that the feeling of isolation in the desert is palpable, making the ride even more special.

**Wildlife:** While the desert may appear barren, it is home to a variety of wildlife. During the ride, travelers may catch glimpses of desert-adapted animals like oryx, springbok, and ostriches. The experience provides a unique opportunity to see how wildlife survives in such a harsh environment.

**The Skeleton Coast:** Depending on the flight route, some hot air balloon rides might venture close to the **Skeleton Coast**—a stretch of rugged coastline famous for shipwrecks, desert dunes meeting the ocean, and misty mornings. The contrast between the desert and the sea is particularly striking from the air.

**4. The Hot Air Balloon Ride Experience:**

**Pre-flight Preparations:** Balloon rides typically begin before dawn, when guests arrive at the launch site and are given a briefing. Watching the balloon being inflated is a spectacle in itself.

**Duration:** The ride usually lasts between **45 minutes to 1.5 hours**, providing ample time to take in the beauty of the landscape.

**Post-flight Celebrations:** After landing, a celebratory toast with champagne often marks the end of the experience, a perfect way to reflect on the breathtaking adventure.

## Quad Biking in the Namib Desert

The **Namib Desert**, the world's oldest desert, spans Namibia's western coast and offers an unparalleled adventure for visitors. Quad biking across the endless dunes is an exhilarating experience that combines speed, skill, and scenic beauty.

**What to Expect**

**Dune Exploration**: Riders navigate through towering sand dunes, some reaching heights of over 300 meters, providing breathtaking views of the desert landscape.

**Thrilling Rides:** The varying slopes and ridges offer both high-speed thrills and technical riding challenges, making it an adventure suited for both beginners and experienced riders.

**Eco-Friendly Adventures**: Many tour operators emphasize environmental responsibility, following designated trails to minimize damage to the delicate desert ecosystem.

**Wildlife Encounters**: Though the desert appears barren, it is home to fascinating wildlife, including oryx, springbok, jackals, and smaller creatures like geckos and chameleons.

### Best Places for Quad Biking in Namibia

**Swakopmund**: The adventure capital of Namibia, offering guided quad biking tours through the dramatic dunes of the Namib Desert.

**Walvis Bay**: Known for its stunning coastal views and the famous **Dune 7**, one of the highest dunes in Namibia.

**Sossusvlei**: While less common for quad biking, this area's red dunes create an unforgettable riding experience.

## Camping & Overlanding Safaris

Camping and overlanding safaris in **Botswana and Namibia** allow travelers to experience the raw beauty of the African wilderness, sleeping under the stars while exploring vast national parks, deserts, and wildlife reserves. Overlanding—traveling in rugged, self-sufficient vehicles—offers an adventurous and flexible way to explore remote areas.

### What to Expect

**Bush Camping Under the Stars**: Many campsites are located in the heart of national parks, offering an authentic wilderness experience with no fences—just nature and wildlife around you.

**Self-Drive or Guided Expeditions**: Travelers can choose between fully guided tours with expert guides or self-drive overlanding adventures in equipped 4x4 vehicles.

**Cooking Over an Open Fire**: Meals are often prepared over an open flame, enhancing the outdoor experience with traditional bush cooking.

**Up-Close Wildlife Encounters**: Many campsites are in prime wildlife areas where animals roam freely. It's not uncommon to hear lions roaring at night or see elephants near your campsite.

### Best Locations for Camping & Overlanding Safaris

### Botswana

**Okavango Delta**: Offers unique water-based camping experiences in mokoro (canoe) safaris and island campsites.

**Chobe National Park**: Known for large elephant herds and incredible wildlife sightings. Camping here provides direct access to game-rich areas.

**Central Kalahari Game Reserve**: A remote and wild destination, perfect for adventurous travelers seeking solitude and stunning desert landscapes.

### Namibia

**Etosha National Park**: Famous for its waterholes that attract diverse wildlife, making it one of Africa's top camping destinations.

**Skeleton Coast**: A surreal, rugged coastal area with shipwrecks, dunes, and incredible scenery.

**Damaraland**: A remote wilderness area with unique landscapes and desert-adapted elephants.

## Kayaking & Dolphin Watching in Walvis Bay

Walvis Bay, located on Namibia's coast, is famous for its marine life and offers **kayaking adventures** combined with **dolphin watching** for a more intimate wildlife experience. Unlike boat tours, kayaking allows for a **closer and quieter** interaction with nature, making it a must-do activity.

### What to Expect

**Paddle Through Calm Waters**: The sheltered bay offers relatively smooth waters, making it accessible for beginners and experienced kayakers alike.

**Up-Close Dolphin Encounters**: The bay is home to **bottlenose, dusky, and Heaviside's dolphins**, which often swim alongside kayaks, putting on playful displays.

**Cape Fur Seals**: Kayakers can paddle near Pelican Point, where thousands of **Cape fur seals** gather. These curious creatures often approach kayaks and may even swim alongside them.

**Bird Watching**: Walvis Bay is a prime spot for spotting flamingos, pelicans, and cormorants along the shallow lagoons.

**Eco-Friendly Adventure**: Kayaking has minimal environmental impact, making it one of the most sustainable ways to explore the bay.

**Best Time to Visit**

**September to April**: Warmer weather and increased wildlife activity.

**June to August**: Cooler temperatures but excellent dolphin-watching opportunities.

**Best Kayaking Locations**

**Pelican Point**: A prime location for seeing seals, dolphins, and seabirds.

**Walvis Bay Lagoon**: Ideal for calmer waters and birdwatching.

## Hiking Trails & Multi-Day Treks

For outdoor enthusiasts, Botswana and Namibia offer breathtaking hiking opportunities, from short scenic trails to challenging multi-day treks. These hikes provide an immersive way to explore stunning landscapes, from Namibia's desert mountains to Botswana's savannahs and gorges.

**What to Expect**

**Diverse Terrain**: Hikers can experience everything from rolling sand dunes and rocky canyons to lush river valleys.

**Wildlife Encounters**: Some trails pass through conservation areas where hikers may spot antelope, zebras, and even predators from a safe distance.

**Cultural Insights**: Many treks lead through areas inhabited by indigenous groups, such as the San Bushmen, offering cultural experiences alongside nature.

**Remote, Off-the-Grid Experiences**: Multi-day treks often require **camping under the stars**, making for a raw and rewarding outdoor adventure.

## Best Hiking Locations

### Namibia

**Fish River Canyon Trail** (85 km, 4-5 days) – One of Africa's most famous hikes, leading through the **second-largest canyon in the world**.

**Waterberg Plateau Trails** (various distances) – Offers scenic hikes through lush plateaus with excellent wildlife viewing.

**Naukluft Mountains Trail** (120 km, 8 days) – A demanding trek with breathtaking desert and mountain views.

### Botswana

**Tsodilo Hills Trails** – A shorter, cultural hike featuring ancient **San rock art** and sacred landscapes.

**Tswapong Hills** – A scenic hike through lush vegetation, waterfalls, and historical sites.

### Best Time to Hike

**May to September** (Dry season) – Cooler temperatures and ideal conditions for hiking.

**Avoid December to February** – Extremely hot, especially in desert regions.

# Chapter 7: Culture, History & Local Life

## Indigenous Tribes: San Bushmen, Himba & Herero

### 1. The San Bushmen (Basarwa)

The San Bushmen, one of the world's oldest surviving cultures, are indigenous hunter-gatherers who have lived in Botswana and Namibia for thousands of years. They have an intimate knowledge of nature and have adapted to some of Africa's harshest environments, such as the Kalahari Desert.

**Cultural Highlights**

**Tracking & Survival Skills**: The San people are expert trackers and use traditional methods to hunt and gather food. Visitors can join them on guided bush walks to learn about medicinal plants, animal tracking, and survival techniques.

**Click Language**: The San speak languages rich in **click sounds**, a linguistic feature unique to their culture.

**Rock Art**: Ancient **San rock paintings**, found in places like **Tsodilo Hills (Botswana) and Twyfelfontein (Namibia)**, depict their spiritual beliefs and hunting traditions.

**Storytelling & Dance**: They pass down their history through oral storytelling and mesmerizing trance dances used for healing and connecting with the spiritual world.

**Where to Experience the San Culture**

**D'Kar & Ghanzi, Botswana** – Visitors can interact with San communities and witness their traditional lifestyle.

**Tsumkwe, Namibia** – Home to some of Namibia's remaining San communities, offering guided cultural experiences.

**Tsodilo Hills, Botswana** – A UNESCO World Heritage Site with over **4,500 ancient rock paintings**.

## 2. The Himba People

The Himba are a semi-nomadic, pastoral tribe mainly residing in northern Namibia, particularly in the Kunene Region. They are known for their distinctive red ochre body paint, intricate hairstyles, and traditional way of life.

### Cultural Highlights

**Red Ochre Body Paint**: Himba women apply a mixture of **butterfat, red ochre, and aromatic herbs** (otjize) on their skin, giving them a unique reddish hue. This serves as **protection against the sun and insects** and is a symbol of beauty.

**Elaborate Hairstyles**: Hairstyles indicate age, social status, and marital status. Young girls wear braided styles, while married women and elders have elaborate headdresses.

**Cattle & Wealth**: Cattle are central to Himba culture, serving as a measure of wealth and status.

**Traditional Villages**: The Himba live in **circular huts** made from wood, dung, and mud, maintaining their **traditional lifestyle despite modern influences**.

### Where to Experience the Himba Culture

**Opuwo, Namibia** – The gateway to Himba villages, offering authentic cultural visits.

**Kaokoland, Namibia** – A remote area where visitors can engage with Himba communities.

## 3. The Herero People

The Herero people, originally cattle herders, are found in Namibia and Botswana. Unlike the semi-nomadic Himba, they have embraced modernity while preserving many traditions. They are best known for their Victorian-era dresses, a legacy of German colonial influence.

### Cultural Highlights

**Traditional Dress**: Herero women wear **long, voluminous dresses** with petticoats and a **horn-shaped headdress**, symbolizing cattle horns.

**Historical Resilience**: The Herero suffered **genocide under German colonial rule (1904-1908)**. Today, their annual **Herero Day** commemorates their history and resilience.

**Cattle Culture**: Like the Himba, cattle remain central to Herero identity.

**Language**: They speak **Otjiherero**, a Bantu language.

**Where to Experience the Herero Culture**

**Okahandja, Namibia** – Hosts the **Herero Day celebrations**, an important cultural event.

**Central & Eastern Namibia** – Where many Herero communities reside.

## Traditional Music & Dance

Both Botswana and Namibia have rich musical traditions that reflect their diverse cultures. Traditional music and dance play an important role in storytelling, spiritual rituals, and celebrations.

### 1. San Bushmen Music & Dance

**Healing Trance Dance**: The San perform rhythmic trance dances, often around a fire, as a spiritual practice to heal the sick and connect with ancestors.

**Instruments**: Traditional **bow instruments** and **handclapping** accompany their dances.

### 2. Himba & Herero Music

**Himba Chanting**: The Himba use rhythmic **chanting and clapping** in communal gatherings and celebrations.

**Herero Singing**: The Herero sing in choirs, blending **Christian hymns** with traditional melodies.

### 3. Tswana & Setswana Music (Botswana)

**Traditional Dances**:

**Setapa** – A rhythmic dance performed during celebrations.

**Gumboot Dance** – Originally performed by miners, now a cultural dance in Botswana.

**Instruments:**

**Segaba** – A single-stringed fiddle played in traditional Botswana music.

**Marimbas & Drums** – Used in both Botswana and Namibia for festive occasions.

### 4. Owambo & Damara Music (Namibia)

**Damara "Click" Songs**: The Damara people incorporate **click sounds** into their singing.

**Oviritje Music**: A modern blend of **traditional Namibian rhythms** and contemporary beats, popular among the Ovaherero.

### Where to Experience Traditional Music & Dance

**Maun, Botswana** – Cultural performances at lodges and local villages.

**Windhoek, Namibia** – Cultural centers host traditional dance performances.

**San Villages (Botswana & Namibia)** – Visitors can witness trance dances firsthand.

## Colonial History & Independence Movements

### Botswana: From Protectorate to Independence

**Colonial Rule**: Botswana was a **British protectorate known as Bechuanaland** from 1885 to 1966. Unlike other African territories, it was not a formal colony but was still under British control.

**Seretse Khama & Independence**: Botswana gained independence peacefully in **1966**, led by **Sir Seretse Khama**, who became the country's first president. His policies helped build Botswana into one of Africa's most stable democracies.

**Minimal Colonial Influence**: Unlike Namibia, Botswana did not experience significant European settlement, allowing it to maintain much of its cultural identity.

### Namibia: A Struggle for Liberation

**German Colonial Rule (1884–1915)**: Namibia was part of **German South West Africa**, during which **brutal conflicts** occurred, including the **Herero and Nama genocide (1904–1908)**, where tens of thousands were killed.

**South African Occupation (1915–1990)**: After Germany's defeat in **World War I**, South Africa took control, enforcing **apartheid policies** that oppressed indigenous Namibians.

**SWAPO & Armed Resistance**: The **South West Africa People's Organization (SWAPO)** led an armed struggle against South African rule from **1966 to 1990**, with support from Angola, the Soviet Union, and Cuba.

**Independence in 1990**: After years of conflict and international pressure, Namibia gained independence in **1990**, with **Sam Nujoma** as its first president.

**Colonial Landmarks & Museums to Visit**

**Botswana National Museum (Gaborone, Botswana)** – Showcases Botswana's pre-colonial and post-independence history.

**Independence Memorial Museum (Windhoek, Namibia)** – Documents Namibia's long struggle for freedom.

**Tintenpalast (Windhoek, Namibia)** – A former German colonial administrative building, now Namibia's Parliament.

**Swakopmund (Namibia)** – A coastal town with preserved **German colonial architecture**, giving insight into Namibia's European past.

# Art, Handicrafts & Local Markets

Botswana and Namibia have rich artistic traditions, with skilled artisans creating handmade crafts, textiles, jewelry, and paintings that reflect their cultures and histories.

## Botswana: Basket Weaving & Traditional Crafts

**Okavango Delta Baskets**: Considered some of Africa's finest, these are woven from **mokola palm leaves** and dyed using natural pigments.

**Leatherwork & Beadwork**: The San Bushmen craft intricate **beaded jewelry and leather accessories**, often used in traditional ceremonies.

**Wood Carvings**: Makgadikgadi craftsmen create **animal figurines and walking sticks**, often depicting wildlife.

## Namibia: Textiles, Pottery & Stone Carvings

**Himba Jewelry & Body Adornments**: Made from copper, shells, and beads, Himba jewelry is highly symbolic.

**San Rock Art**: Ancient petroglyphs can be seen at sites like **Twyfelfontein (a UNESCO World Heritage Site)**, featuring prehistoric paintings of animals and hunting scenes.

**Mahangu Baskets**: Made by Kavango women, these baskets are used for storing millet and other grains.

## Best Local Markets & Art Centers

**Ghanzi Craft Market (Botswana)** – Features authentic San crafts, including bow-and-arrow sets and ostrich eggshell jewelry.

**Windhoek Craft Market (Namibia)** – A great place for handmade leather goods, woven baskets, and hand-painted textiles.

**Swakopmund Arts Association (Namibia)** – Showcases local artists, including painters and sculptors.

**Okavango Craft Brewery & Market (Maun, Botswana)** – A fusion of arts, crafts, and locally brewed beer.

# Cultural Festivals & Events

**1. Maitsong Festival**

**Where**: Gaborone, Botswana

**When**: March/April

**What to Expect**:

Botswana's **largest performing arts festival**, featuring **theater, dance, music, and poetry**.

A mix of **local and international artists**, offering a platform for creative expression.

Hosted at the **Maitisong Theatre**, with performances also held in open-air venues, schools, and community centers.

**2. Dithubaruba Cultural Festival**

**Where**: Molepolole, Botswana

**When**: September

**What to Expect**:

Celebrates the **heritage of the Bakwena people**, one of Botswana's major ethnic groups.

Features **traditional music, dance, poetry, and storytelling**.

Offers insight into **pre-colonial history, oral traditions, and Kgotla (tribal council) discussions**.

**3. Khawa Dune Challenge & Cultural Festival**

**Where**: Khawa, Kgalagadi Desert, Botswana

**When**: May

**What to Expect**:

A combination of **adventure sports (quad biking, off-road racing)** and **traditional Setswana music and dance**.

Celebrates **desert culture** with food stalls, art displays, and cultural exhibitions.

### 4. President's Day Celebrations

**Where**: Nationwide, Botswana

**When**: July

**What to Expect**:

A national holiday celebrating Botswana's unity and progress.

Showcases **traditional Setswana music, dance, and fashion**.

Includes **arts and crafts competitions**, with winners displaying their work at the **National Art Exhibition**.

## Cultural Festivals & Events in Namibia

### 1. Windhoek Karneval (WIKA)

**Where**: Windhoek, Namibia

**When**: March/April

**What to Expect**:

Namibia's biggest **German cultural festival**, influenced by the country's colonial history.

Features **parades, masquerade balls, music performances, and carnival floats**.

A unique mix of **German and Namibian traditions**, with lively street celebrations.

### 2. Oshituthi Shomagongo – Marula Festival (UNESCO Cultural Heritage)

**Where**: Northern Namibia (Oshiwambo communities)

**When**: March/April

**What to Expect**:

A festival centered around the **marula fruit**, which is fermented into a traditional drink.

A communal event where **Oshiwambo tribes** gather to celebrate unity, storytelling, and music.

Recognized by **UNESCO** as an **intangible cultural heritage event**.

### 3. Herero Day

**Where**: Okahandja, Namibia

**When**: August 26

**What to Expect**:

A commemoration of **Herero leaders and warriors** who resisted German colonial rule.

Features **parades of Herero people dressed in Victorian-style attire**, a tradition passed down from German colonial influences.

Includes **ceremonial rituals, historical speeches, and traditional feasts**.

### 4. Namibia Independence Day

**Where**: Nationwide, Namibia

**When**: March 21

**What to Expect**:

A national celebration of Namibia's **independence from South African rule (1990)**.

Large-scale parades, fireworks, music festivals, and cultural performances.

Major celebrations in **Windhoek**, with events also held in smaller towns.

### 5. Kuste Karneval (Coastal Carnival)

**Where**: Swakopmund, Namibia

**When**: August

**What to Expect**:

A lively **coastal festival** combining Namibian and German traditions.

Features **street performances, comedy shows, beer gardens, and costume parties**.

Reflects Swakopmund's **unique colonial heritage and modern cultural fusion**.

**Why Attend These Festivals?**

**Cultural Immersion**: Experience traditional music, dance, food, and storytelling.

**Meet Indigenous Communities**: Interact with San Bushmen, Herero, Himba, and Oshiwambo people.

**Support Local Artisans**: Purchase handmade crafts, textiles, and jewelry at festival markets.

**Learn History Firsthand**: Gain insights into colonial struggles, independence movements, and tribal customs.

# Chapter 8: Food & Dining Experiences

## Traditional Dishes & Street Food

1. Seswaa (Botswana) / Oshifima and Ombidi (Namibia)

Seswaa is Botswana's national dish, a slow-cooked, shredded beef or goat dish enjoyed at celebrations and daily meals. In Namibia, a similar dish, Oshifima (a thick maize porridge), is commonly served with Ombidi (wild spinach) and meat stews.

**Main Ingredients:**

**Seswaa:** Beef or goat, water, salt

**Oshifima & Ombidi:** Maize meal, wild spinach, meat

**Taste:**

**Seswaa:** Tender, slightly salty, and rich in natural beef flavors

**Oshifima & Ombidi:** Hearty, earthy, and slightly bitter from the spinach

**Preparation:**

**Seswaa:** Meat is boiled for several hours until tender, then pounded or shredded with salt.

**Oshifima & Ombidi:** Maize meal is stirred into boiling water until thick, while the spinach is cooked with onions and sometimes mixed with meat or peanut butter.

**Where to Try:**

**Botswana:** The Boma in Gaborone, roadside stalls, and family gatherings.

**Namibia:** Joe's Beerhouse (Windhoek), local shebeens (beer halls), and village kitchens.

**What Makes It Iconic?**

Seswaa is deeply tied to Botswana's communal traditions, often served at weddings and national holidays. Oshifima is a staple food that sustains Namibian households, showcasing local grains and foraged greens.

**Tips for Enjoying:**

Eat with your hands for an authentic experience.

Pair with Morogo (wild spinach) or a cold local beer.

Try it with spicy chili sauce for added flavor.

## 2. Kapana (Namibia) & Mokoto (Botswana)

Kapana is Namibia's beloved street food—grilled beef strips served with spice blends. Mokoto, a Botswanan delicacy, is a slow-cooked tripe dish packed with rich, meaty flavors.

**Main Ingredients:**

**Kapana:** Beef, chili powder, spices

**Mokoto:** Tripe (cow intestines), salt, onions, garlic

**Taste:**

**Kapana:** Smoky, spicy, and juicy

**Mokoto:** Chewy, slightly gamey, with a deep umami flavor

**Preparation:**

**Kapana:** Meat is grilled over an open flame, sliced into small pieces, and served with a signature spice mix.

**Mokoto:** Tripe is boiled for hours until tender, sometimes with onions and seasoning.

**Where to Try:**

**Botswana:** Street vendors in Francistown and Gaborone markets.

**Namibia:** Single Quarters Market in Katutura, Windhoek.

**What Makes It Iconic?**

Kapana is an essential part of Namibian street culture, bringing people together at markets. Mokoto is prized for its bold flavors and nutritional value, often eaten for breakfast or as a hangover cure.

**Tips for Enjoying:**

Eat Kapana fresh off the grill with spice rubs and salsas.

Try Mokoto with dumplings or porridge for a complete meal.

Ask vendors for the spiciest Kapana mix for an extra kick.

## 3. Vetkoek (Botswana & Namibia)

Vetkoek, meaning "fat cake," is a deep-fried bread often stuffed with savory or sweet fillings, found across both countries as a popular snack.

**Main Ingredients:**

Flour, yeast, sugar, salt, oil

Fillings: Minced meat, cheese, jam

**Taste:**

Crispy on the outside, fluffy inside, with a balance of savory or sweet depending on the filling.

**Preparation:**

Dough is mixed and left to rise.

Small pieces are deep-fried until golden brown.

Filled with meat, cheese, or enjoyed plain.

### Where to Try:

**Botswana:** Bus stations and local cafes in Gaborone.

**Namibia:** Windhoek's street food stalls and open markets.

### What Makes It Iconic?

Vetkoek is an adaptable comfort food enjoyed by all age groups, blending Dutch colonial influence with local flavors.

### Tips for Enjoying:

Try it fresh and warm for the best texture.

Pair it with boerewors (farm-style sausage) for a filling meal.

Opt for the spicy mince filling for a traditional taste.

## 4. Mahangu Porridge (Namibia) / Bogobe (Botswana)

Mahangu porridge and Bogobe are staple grain-based porridges, often eaten with stews, milk, or sugar, representing the agricultural backbone of both countries.

**Main Ingredients:**

**Mahangu Porridge:** Pearl millet flour, water

**Bogobe:** Sorghum or maize meal, water, milk

**Taste:**

Slightly nutty, mild, with a thick and smooth texture.

**Preparation:**

Flour is mixed into boiling water, stirred until thick.

Served with meat, milk, or sugar.

**Where to Try:**

**Botswana:** Local homes, roadside eateries.

**Namibia:** Northern markets, traditional villages.

**What Makes It Iconic?**

Both porridges are nutrient-dense, historically significant, and deeply tied to indigenous farming traditions.

**Tips for Enjoying:**

Eat with your hands for an authentic experience.

Try it with butter or peanut butter for a richer taste.

Pair with grilled meat for a balanced meal.

5. **Mopane Worms (Botswana & Namibia)**

A high-protein delicacy, Mopane worms (caterpillars of the Emperor Moth) are widely eaten in rural and urban areas, dried, fried, or stewed.

**Main Ingredients:**

Mopane worms, salt, onions, tomatoes, chili

**Taste:**

Chewy, slightly nutty, and meaty with an umami depth.

**Preparation:**

Worms are cleaned and sun-dried.

Rehydrated and cooked with spices or deep-fried.

**Where to Try:**

**Botswana:** Local markets in Maun and Gaborone.

**Namibia:** Katutura Market, rural villages.

**What Makes It Iconic?**

Mopane worms are a sustainable protein source, crucial for rural diets, and a cultural staple with a long history.

**Tips for Enjoying:**

Try them fried for a crispier texture.

Pair with maize porridge for a complete meal.

Don't be hesitant—they're surprisingly delicious!

# Fine Dining & Gourmet Safari Meals

## 1. Luxury Safari Lodges: Bush Dining at Its Best

Many high-end safari lodges in Botswana and Namibia provide **gourmet meals** in breathtaking natural settings. Dining under the stars, enjoying **bush breakfasts, sundowner cocktails, and multi-course dinners** by a campfire is a signature experience.

### What to Expect

**Five-Star Chefs & Fresh Ingredients**: Safari lodges source the finest local and organic ingredients, creating meals that blend African flavors with international techniques.

**Unique Dining Settings**: Enjoy **dinners on a riverbank, private candlelit meals in the dunes, or open-air feasts in the savannah.**

**Signature Safari Dishes:**

**Grilled game meats** like kudu, springbok, and oryx.

**Braaivleis** (Southern African-style barbecue).

**Freshly baked bush bread** served with local preserves.

**Traditional stews**, such as seswaa (slow-cooked beef) or potjiekos (a rich, slow-cooked stew).

### Top Safari Lodges for Gourmet Dining

**Jack's Camp (Botswana)** – Famous for its lavish Persian-style tented dining and **classic bush tea experiences.**

**Zarafa Camp (Botswana)** – Offers **tailor-made fine dining menus** with ingredients sourced from local farms.

**Wolwedans Dune Camp (Namibia)** – Located in the Namib Desert, serving **exquisite gourmet meals with desert views.**

**Onguma The Fort (Namibia)** – A luxurious lodge near Etosha National Park with an **innovative menu combining local and global flavors.**

# Best Local Restaurants & Cafés

For travelers looking to experience **authentic local cuisine** and contemporary African flavors, Botswana and Namibia offer fantastic restaurants and cafés in cities and towns.

**Best Restaurants in Botswana**

**1. The Courtyard (Gaborone)**

A fine-dining restaurant known for its elegant African fusion cuisine.

Serves **grilled meats, fresh seafood, and traditional Botswanan dishes** in a stylish courtyard setting.

**2. Sanitas Tea Garden (Gaborone)**

A **relaxed garden café** serving homemade pastries, teas, and light meals.

Popular for breakfast and lunch, with a peaceful botanical ambiance.

**3. The Beef Baron (Maun)**

Located near the Okavango Delta, it specializes in **premium Botswana beef steaks** and local game meats.

Offers a cozy setting with a fantastic wine selection.

**Best Restaurants in Namibia**

**1. Joe's Beerhouse (Windhoek)**

One of Namibia's most famous restaurants, offering a **rustic atmosphere and a menu featuring game meats** like zebra, crocodile, and oryx.

A must-visit for those wanting a true taste of **Namibian-style barbecue (braai)**.

**2. The Stellenbosch Wine Bar & Bistro (Windhoek)**

A stylish restaurant and wine bar with **South African and European-inspired cuisine**.

Known for its **fine steaks, cheese platters, and excellent wines**.

### 3. The Tug (Swakopmund)

A **seaside restaurant built from an old tugboat**, serving **fresh Atlantic seafood**.

Signature dishes include **Namibian oysters, grilled kingklip, and lobster platters**.

## Wine & Beer Scene in Namibia & Botswana

While **South Africa** is the region's dominant wine producer, **Namibia and Botswana** have emerging wine scenes, strong beer traditions, and a growing interest in **craft brewing and local distilleries**.

### Wine Scene

**Namibia's Unique Vineyards**

Although Namibia's dry desert climate may seem unsuitable for winemaking, the country has a few vineyards producing exceptional wines. The most well-known is:

**Neuras Wine & Wildlife Estate (Namibia)**

Located in the **Namib Desert**, this vineyard is one of the driest wineries in the world.

Produces **Shiraz, Merlot, and Cabernet Sauvignon**, benefiting from underground water sources.

Visitors can enjoy **wine tastings** combined with conservation tours supporting local wildlife.

**Botswana's Wine Culture**

Botswana does not have its own vineyards, but wine is widely available.

The country imports premium wines, primarily from **South Africa's Cape Winelands**, making it easy to find **Pinotage, Chenin Blanc, and Sauvignon Blanc** in high-end lodges and restaurants.

Some **safari lodges** offer curated wine pairings, blending **wild game dishes** with fine wines.

## Beer Scene: Local & Craft Brewing

### Namibia's Beer Culture

Namibia has a strong **beer culture**, heavily influenced by German colonial rule. The country follows the **Reinheitsgebot (German Beer Purity Law)**, ensuring high-quality brewing standards.

**Popular Namibian Beers:**

**Windhoek Lager** – The country's flagship beer, a crisp and refreshing lager brewed with malted barley, hops, and water.

**Tafel Lager** – A slightly maltier and smoother alternative to Windhoek Lager.

**Camelthorn Brewing Company** – Namibia's leading **craft brewery**, producing unique beers such as **Weissbier, Red Ale, and IPA**.

**Where to Experience Namibian Beer:**

**Joe's Beerhouse (Windhoek)** – The best place to try local brews in a lively beer hall atmosphere.

**Swakopmund Breweries** – Offers craft beer tastings and brewery tours.

### Botswana's Beer Culture

Beer is an important social drink in Botswana, with a mix of **commercial lagers and traditional sorghum-based brews**.

**Popular Beers in Botswana:**

**St. Louis Lager** – Botswana's most famous beer, a light and easy-drinking lager.

**Chibuku Shake-Shake** – A traditional **sorghum beer** with a thick texture and slightly sour taste, commonly enjoyed in rural areas.

**Okavango Craft Brewery** – A rising craft brewery producing **artisanal beers using local ingredients**, available in Maun.

**Where to Experience Botswana Beer:**

**Bull & Bush Pub (Gaborone)** – One of Botswana's oldest and most popular pubs, serving local and imported beers.

**Okavango Craft Brewery (Maun)** – A great stop for beer lovers exploring the Okavango Delta.

## Bush Cooking & Braai Culture

Outdoor cooking is an essential part of the culinary traditions in Namibia and Botswana, whether through bush cooking in remote safari locations or braai (barbecue) gatherings with friends and family.

**Bush Cooking: Safari-Style Dining**

**Cooking over an open flame** is a traditional way of preparing food in the wilderness, particularly in **safari lodges and overland tours**.

Meals often include **grilled game meats, stews, and fresh-baked breads** prepared in cast-iron pots over a fire.

Many lodges offer **interactive bush cooking experiences**, allowing guests to learn traditional African cooking techniques.

**Braai Culture: The Ultimate African Barbecue**

The **braai (barbecue) is a major social event** in both countries, similar to South African tradition. Families and friends gather around a fire to **grill meats, enjoy drinks, and share stories**.

**Typical Braai Dishes:**

**Game Meat** – Kudu, springbok, eland, and oryx are commonly grilled.

**Boerewors** – A spiced beef and pork sausage popular across Southern Africa.

**Pap (Maize Porridge)** – A staple side dish served with tomato sauce or meat gravy.

**Vetkoek** – Deep-fried dough filled with minced meat.

**Where to Experience a Traditional Braai:**

**Local lodges and campsites** often organize **braai nights** for guests.

**Etosha National Park (Namibia) and Moremi Game Reserve (Botswana)** allow visitors to have **self-catered braais in designated areas**.

**Cattle Baron (Windhoek, Namibia)** – A top steakhouse serving excellent grilled meats.

**Bimbo's (Gaborone, Botswana)** – A local favorite for barbecue-style meats.

# Chapter 9: Shopping & Souvenirs

## Best Markets for Handcrafted Goods

Markets in Botswana and Namibia are some of the best places to find authentic, locally made crafts. Many items are produced using traditional methods passed down through generations, and purchasing them directly from artisans helps sustain their livelihoods.

**Botswana**

Botswana is known for its high-quality handwoven baskets, wood carvings, and beadwork. Many of these crafts are made by indigenous communities such as the San Bushmen and the Bayei people, who use natural materials sourced from their surroundings.

**Gaborone Craft Market (Gaborone)**

A well-known market in the capital, selling handwoven baskets, wood carvings, beaded jewelry, pottery, and leather goods.

Many of the items come from rural cooperatives, ensuring that artisans receive fair compensation for their work.

Okavango Delta baskets, made with intricate patterns and natural dyes, are among the most sought-after items.

**Maun Art and Craft Centre (Maun)**

Situated near the Okavango Delta, this center specializes in handwoven baskets, carved wooden bowls, and artwork inspired by local wildlife.

Artisans from the Bayei and Hambukushu communities showcase their exceptional weaving techniques, producing baskets that are both decorative and functional.

**Thapong Visual Arts Centre (Gaborone)**

A hub for contemporary Batswana artists, featuring paintings, sculptures, and mixed-media artwork.

Visitors can engage with artists, learn about their creative processes, and purchase unique, one-of-a-kind pieces.

## Namibia

Namibia's markets highlight the craftsmanship of diverse ethnic groups, including the Himba, Herero, and San communities. Many crafts are inspired by Namibia's desert landscapes and rich cultural traditions.

### Namibia Craft Centre (Windhoek)

The largest craft market in Namibia, featuring over 40 stalls selling handmade goods from all over the country.

Best items to buy include handwoven rugs, Himba jewelry, hand-carved wooden bowls, and traditional Namibian textiles.

The center supports women's cooperatives and fair-trade initiatives, making it a great place for ethical shopping.

### Swakopmund Arts and Crafts Market (Swakopmund)

A vibrant market featuring traditional and contemporary Namibian crafts, including wildlife-inspired sculptures, tribal masks, and San rock art replicas.

Swakopmund's coastal influence adds a unique touch to the crafts, with some artisans incorporating seashells and oceanic themes into their designs.

### Okahandja Mbangura Woodcarvers Market (Okahandja)

A major center for wooden carvings, specializing in hand-carved statues, bowls, and animal figurines.

Run by Kavango artisans, known for their expertise in working with mahogany and ebony.

Many of the carvings depict Namibia's iconic wildlife, making them a perfect souvenir for travelers.

# Ethical Souvenir Shopping: What to Buy and What to Avoid

When buying souvenirs, it is important to ensure that items are ethically sourced and that purchases support local artisans rather than mass-produced imports. Ethical shopping helps preserve traditional craftsmanship and promotes sustainability.

## Ethical Purchases

Handwoven baskets, particularly those from the Okavango Delta, made using sustainable palm fibers.

Beaded jewelry crafted by San Bushmen and Himba women, often produced as part of community development projects.

Locally made textiles, including Herero and Damara fabric prints, commonly used in traditional clothing.

Wood carvings made from ethically sourced mahogany, mopane, or jacaranda wood, depicting local wildlife or cultural motifs.

Handmade pottery featuring traditional African patterns and techniques.

Leather goods, such as sandals and bags, crafted using local materials.

## Items to Avoid

Souvenirs made from endangered wildlife, such as ivory, tortoiseshell, or animal pelts, which contribute to poaching and environmental degradation.

Mass-produced trinkets imported from outside Africa, which do not support local artisans.

Items made from protected tree species or unsustainably harvested wood.

Fake "traditional" crafts that lack cultural authenticity and are not made by local communities.

## Tips for Ethical Shopping

Buy directly from artisans or cooperatives to ensure fair compensation.

Ask about the origin of materials and whether they were ethically sourced.

Support fair-trade markets and community-run craft centers.

Avoid aggressive bargaining, as many artisans already price their work fairly based on the time and effort involved.

Look for certifications or guarantees of authenticity when purchasing high-value crafts.

## Famous Botswana & Namibian Gems & Jewelry

Both Botswana and Namibia are important sources of precious and semi-precious stones, with a strong tradition of jewelry making. Botswana is world-famous for its diamond industry, while Namibia is known for its semi-precious stones such as amethyst, tourmaline, and aquamarine.

**Botswana's Diamond Industry**

Botswana is one of the top diamond producers in the world, with its mines yielding some of the highest-quality stones. The country is a leader in ethical mining, ensuring that its diamond industry benefits local communities and supports economic growth. The most significant mines include:

**Jwaneng Diamond Mine** – Considered the world's richest diamond mine in terms of value, producing some of the finest stones.

**Orapa Diamond Mine** – The largest diamond mine by area, located in northern Botswana, producing vast quantities of high-quality diamonds.

Visitors interested in purchasing diamonds can explore reputable jewelers in Botswana's major cities, particularly in Gaborone. Stores such as De Beers Diamond Jewelers and KGK Diamonds offer expertly cut stones, set in elegant and modern designs. Some safari lodges also arrange private diamond-buying experiences, where guests can learn about the sourcing and certification process before purchasing a piece.

**Namibia's Semi-Precious Stones and Jewelry**

Namibia is known for its wealth of semi-precious gemstones, many of which are mined in the Erongo region and the Skeleton Coast. These stones are often crafted into jewelry by local artisans and set in gold or silver. Some of the most famous gemstones from Namibia include:

**Tanzanite** – Though mainly associated with Tanzania, some deposits are found in Namibia, known for their deep blue-violet hues.

**Tourmaline** – Found in a variety of colors, including green, pink, and the rare watermelon tourmaline, which has a mix of pink and green shades in a single crystal.

**Aquamarine** – Mined in the Erongo Mountains, this light blue gemstone is popular in elegant jewelry designs.

**Amethyst** – Namibia produces high-quality deep purple amethyst, particularly from the Brandberg region.

**Tiger's Eye** – A golden-brown stone with a silky sheen, used in beaded bracelets and pendants.

Windhoek, Swakopmund, and Lüderitz are some of the best places to find gemstone jewelry. The Namibia Craft Centre in Windhoek is a popular destination for those looking to buy authentic, locally made jewelry, often created by indigenous artisans.

## Leather, Textiles, and Wood Carvings

Beyond gemstones, Botswana and Namibia also produce fine leather goods, traditional textiles, and wooden artworks, often crafted using time-honored techniques.

### Leather Goods in Botswana and Namibia

Both countries are known for producing high-quality leather, often sourced from kudu, ostrich, and cowhide. These materials are transformed into fashionable and durable accessories such as handbags, belts, wallets, and shoes.

**Kudu Leather** – This soft yet durable leather is widely used for making premium bags, boots, and jackets. It is often left in its natural color or dyed for a more stylish look.

**Ostrich Leather** – Considered a luxury material, ostrich leather is known for its distinctive texture and is used in high-end handbags, wallets, and boots. Namibia, in particular, has a strong tradition of ostrich farming and leather production.

**Cowhide Products** – Cowhide is used for making rugs, cushion covers, and even decorative wall hangings. These products are commonly found in craft markets and boutique stores.

One of the most sustainable projects in Namibia is the Kalahari Wild Silk initiative, which blends locally produced silk with leather to create eco-friendly accessories. Windhoek, Swakopmund, and Gaborone have shops specializing in high-quality leather goods, where travelers can purchase ethically sourced products.

**Traditional Textiles and Fabrics**

Textiles play an important role in the cultural identity of Botswana and Namibia, with many communities incorporating traditional patterns and techniques into their fabrics. Some of the most popular textiles include:

**Herero and Damara Fabrics** – These fabrics feature bold colors and geometric patterns, often used in traditional dresses and decorative textiles. The Herero women, in particular, wear brightly colored dresses with structured headdresses, a style that dates back to the 19th century.

**San Bushmen Beaded Garments** – The San people are known for their intricate beadwork, which is used to decorate clothing and accessories such as purses and belts.

**Handwoven Tapestries** – Some artisan collectives, particularly in Namibia, create woven wall hangings that depict scenes of village life, wildlife, and traditional ceremonies.

Many of these fabrics and garments are available at local markets, such as the Namibia Craft Centre in Windhoek and the Gaborone Craft Market. These venues support fair-trade initiatives, ensuring that artisans receive fair wages for their work.

**Wood Carvings and Sculptures**

Wood carving is a traditional craft in both Botswana and Namibia, with artisans producing everything from small figurines to large decorative sculptures. The wood used in these carvings often comes from sustainable sources, ensuring that the craft does not contribute to deforestation.

**Okavango Delta Wooden Bowls** – These handcrafted bowls, made by the Bayei people of Botswana, are often used for food preparation and serving. They are carved from indigenous woods and feature intricate patterns.

**Kavango Woodcarvings** – The Kavango people of Namibia are known for their skill in creating detailed sculptures, masks, and furniture pieces. Many of these carvings depict wildlife such as elephants, giraffes, and lions.

**Traditional Tribal Masks** – Used in cultural ceremonies, these masks are often carved from wood and decorated with beads, shells, and natural pigments. Some markets sell replicas for decorative purposes.

The Okahandja Mbangura Woodcarvers Market in Namibia is one of the best places to find authentic wooden carvings, where artisans showcase their craftsmanship and allow visitors to see the carving process firsthand.

**Where to Shop for Ethical Souvenirs**

To ensure that purchases support local communities and are ethically sourced, travelers should consider shopping at markets and craft centers that promote fair trade and sustainability. Some of the best places to buy authentic, responsibly made crafts include:

**Namibia Craft Centre (Windhoek)** – A hub for handmade jewelry, leather goods, textiles, and carvings, supporting women's cooperatives and indigenous artisans.

**Gaborone Craft Market (Botswana)** – A great place to buy baskets, wood carvings, and beadwork directly from artisans.

**Okahandja Mbangura Woodcarvers Market (Namibia)** – Specializes in high-quality wooden sculptures made from sustainable materials.

**Maun Art and Craft Centre (Botswana)** – Features handwoven baskets, paintings, and traditional clothing.

# Where to Buy Local Art

Art in Botswana and Namibia is deeply rooted in cultural traditions, storytelling, and nature. From San rock art-inspired paintings and wood carvings to contemporary African art, these countries offer a diverse selection of pieces for collectors and travelers.

## Best Places to Buy Art in Botswana

### Thapong Visual Arts Centre (Gaborone)

A leading hub for **contemporary Botswana artists**, showcasing paintings, sculptures, and mixed-media works.

Visitors can meet artists, view exhibitions, and purchase original artwork directly from the creators.

### Gaborone Craft Market (Gaborone)

Features handmade paintings, woven baskets, and small-scale sculptures by local artisans.

A great place to find **traditional and modern art pieces** at reasonable prices.

### Maun Art and Craft Centre (Maun)

Located near the Okavango Delta, this center focuses on **wildlife and nature-inspired art**.

Works include **watercolor paintings, wood carvings, and decorative textiles**.

### Nhabe Museum (Maun)

A cultural center displaying traditional and modern Botswana artwork.

Offers a small shop selling **locally made paintings and crafts**.

## Best Places to Buy Art in Namibia

### Namibia Craft Centre (Windhoek)

A premier destination for handmade **textiles, wood carvings, jewelry, and paintings**.

Supports local artists and fair-trade initiatives, ensuring ethical sourcing.

### The Project Room (Windhoek)

A contemporary art gallery featuring **modern Namibian artists** working in painting, sculpture, and mixed media.

Often hosts exhibitions and workshops.

### Swakopmund Art Association Gallery (Swakopmund)

Specializes in **landscape paintings, wildlife art, and handcrafted ceramics**.

A great spot to purchase authentic Namibian artwork.

### Lüderitz Art Gallery (Lüderitz)

Showcases **ocean-inspired art, jewelry, and sculptures** crafted by local artisans.

# Chapter 10: Sustainable & Responsible Travel

## Eco-Lodges & Conservation Efforts

Both Botswana and Namibia have embraced sustainable tourism, with **eco-lodges, conservation projects, and community-driven initiatives** playing a major role in protecting wildlife and the environment.

**Eco-Lodges in Botswana**

**Wilderness Mombo Camp (Okavango Delta)**

A luxury eco-lodge in one of Botswana's most biodiverse areas.

Supports **rhino conservation** and operates with **solar energy and eco-friendly water systems**.

**Chobe Game Lodge (Chobe National Park)**

Botswana's only **fully electric safari lodge**, using solar-powered boats and game vehicles.

Strong focus on **women empowerment** in the safari industry.

**Gunn's Camp (Okavango Delta)**

A classic safari camp with **minimal environmental impact**, blending into the natural surroundings.

Supports **sustainable tourism and wildlife monitoring programs**.

**Eco-Lodges in Namibia**

**Wolwedans (NamibRand Nature Reserve)**

A stunning desert retreat promoting **low-impact tourism**.

Runs **conservation programs** to protect the fragile Namib Desert ecosystem.

### Desert Rhino Camp (Damaraland)

Focuses on **black rhino conservation** in partnership with the **Save the Rhino Trust**.

Supports local **Himba and Herero communities**.

### Hoanib Skeleton Coast Camp (Skeleton Coast National Park)

Operates on **solar power** and works closely with researchers to study **desert-adapted elephants and lions**.

## Ethical Wildlife Tourism

### Principles of Ethical Wildlife Tourism

### Respect for Wildlife & Their Natural Behavior

Ethical tours ensure that animals are observed **without interference**, maintaining their natural behaviors.

Safaris should follow strict **viewing distance guidelines**, avoiding activities that involve feeding, touching, or forcing animals into unnatural settings.

### Support for Conservation & Anti-Poaching Efforts

Choosing **lodges, guides, and tour operators** that actively support conservation helps fund **anti-poaching patrols and wildlife rehabilitation**.

Many eco-lodges invest in **reforestation, habitat restoration, and wildlife monitoring**.

### Eco-Friendly Practices & Sustainable Tourism

Ethical safari camps prioritize **solar power, water conservation, and waste reduction**.

Tourists should opt for **low-impact activities**, such as **walking safaris, canoe trips, and electric vehicle safaris**, which reduce carbon footprints.

### Support for Local Communities & Indigenous Knowledge

Ethical tourism ensures that **local communities benefit from wildlife conservation** through employment, education, and sustainable business opportunities.

Visitors should choose operators that **partner with indigenous groups**, such as the **San Bushmen in Botswana and the Himba in Namibia**, for guided nature walks and cultural insights.

### Ethical Wildlife Experiences in Botswana

### Game Drives in the Okavango Delta

Botswana enforces a **low-volume, high-cost tourism model**, reducing environmental strain while funding conservation.

The **Moremi Game Reserve** and private concessions offer ethical game drives with trained guides who prioritize **animal welfare and responsible viewing distances**.

### Walking Safaris in the Kalahari

Led by **San Bushmen trackers**, these safaris provide an **eco-friendly, non-invasive** way to experience the bush while learning about **indigenous survival techniques**.

The Central Kalahari Game Reserve (CKGR) offers **low-impact, foot-based wildlife experiences** that respect both culture and conservation.

### Chobe River Boat Safaris

Unlike traditional game drives, electric boat safaris in **Chobe National Park** allow for a **silent, low-impact** way to view elephants, hippos, and crocodiles.

Operators like **Chobe Game Lodge** use **solar-powered boats** to minimize pollution and disturbance.

### Rhino Conservation at Khama Rhino Sanctuary

A **community-run wildlife project** dedicated to protecting Botswana's **critically endangered white and black rhinos**.

Offers guided safaris focused on **education, conservation, and anti-poaching initiatives**.

## Ethical Wildlife Experiences in Namibia

### Etosha National Park Self-Drive Safaris

Namibia promotes **self-drive safaris**, which reduce the environmental impact of mass tourism.

Strict park rules **prevent off-road driving** and **ensure minimal disruption to wildlife**.

### Desert-Adapted Elephant Tracking in Damaraland

Unlike traditional elephant safaris, this experience follows **desert-adapted elephants in their natural habitat**.

Guides track elephants **without disturbing family groups** and educate visitors on conservation challenges.

### Cheetah Conservation at Okonjima & AfriCat Foundation

Visitors can support **cheetah rescue, rehabilitation, and research** efforts.

No hands-on interaction is allowed, ensuring that animals maintain **wild instincts**.

### Marine Conservation & Dolphin Watching in Walvis Bay

Ethical **dolphin and seal-watching tours** operate with **strict no-chase and no-touch policies**.

Operators use **eco-friendly catamarans**, limiting noise and water pollution.

### How Tourists Can Support Ethical Wildlife Tourism

**Choose Responsible Tour Operators** – Look for safaris accredited by conservation organizations such as **EcoTourism Botswana** and **Namibia's Sustainable Tourism Charter**.

**Avoid Animal Exploitation** – Avoid any activity that allows **petting, riding, or captive animal interactions**, such as lion cub petting or cheetah walks.

**Respect Park Rules & Local Guidelines** – Stick to **designated trails**, keep a safe distance from wildlife, and **never feed animals**.

**Support Conservation Efforts** – Donate to or visit **wildlife sanctuaries and anti-poaching initiatives** that focus on rehabilitation rather than entertainment.

**Stay in Eco-Lodges** – Opt for accommodations that prioritize **sustainability, local employment, and conservation funding.**

## Supporting Local Communities

Tourism is a major source of income for many communities in Botswana and Namibia. Ethical tourism ensures that **local people benefit from conservation, cultural heritage, and hospitality industries** while preserving their traditional lifestyles.

**Ways to Support Local Communities**

**Stay at Community-Owned Lodges & Camps**

Many lodges and camps are **community-managed**, meaning profits go directly to local villages.

Examples:

**Dqãe Qare San Lodge (Botswana)** – A San Bushmen-owned eco-lodge in the Kalahari offering cultural experiences.

**Nkasa Lupala Tented Lodge (Namibia)** – A community-run safari camp near Nkasa Rupara National Park.

**Book Tours with Local Guides**

Hiring **local guides** not only enhances your experience with **firsthand cultural knowledge** but also ensures that **income stays within the community**.

Indigenous groups such as the **San Bushmen, Himba, and Herero** offer guided walks, tracking experiences, and storytelling sessions.

**Buy Locally Made Handicrafts**

Purchasing **authentic, handmade crafts** from markets and cooperatives directly supports **local artisans**.

Best places to buy:

**Namibia Craft Centre (Windhoek)** – Features fair-trade crafts, jewelry, and textiles.

**Gaborone Craft Market (Botswana)** – Offers woven baskets, beaded jewelry, and hand-carved wooden art.

### Dine at Locally Owned Restaurants & Food Markets

Opting for **family-owned restaurants** helps small businesses thrive and provides an opportunity to experience **traditional cuisine**.

Some of the best places include:

**Xwama Traditional Restaurant (Windhoek, Namibia)** – Serves indigenous dishes like kapana (grilled meat).

**Sanitas Tea Garden (Gaborone, Botswana)** – A community-run café offering fresh, organic meals.

### Contribute to Community-Based Conservation Initiatives

Many wildlife conservancies employ local people, providing sustainable livelihoods while protecting nature.

Examples:

**Khama Rhino Sanctuary (Botswana)** – A community-led project that safeguards endangered rhinos.

**Nyae Nyae Conservancy (Namibia)** – Managed by the San Bushmen, focusing on traditional conservation methods.

# Minimizing Your Carbon Footprint

Traveling responsibly in Botswana and Namibia means reducing environmental impact by making **eco-conscious choices**. Both countries have vast, fragile ecosystems, and tourism can have a significant footprint if not managed sustainably.

**Ways to Reduce Your Carbon Footprint While Traveling**

**Choose Eco-Friendly Lodges & Camps**

Look for **solar-powered accommodations, water-saving systems, and plastic-free policies**.

Examples:

**Wilderness Mombo Camp (Botswana)** – 100% solar-powered with a strong focus on conservation.

**Wolwedans Dunes Lodge (Namibia)** – Operates on solar energy and follows strict eco-guidelines.

**Use Sustainable Transportation**

**Opt for electric safari vehicles, walking safaris, or canoe trips** instead of fuel-powered game drives.

In Namibia, **self-drive travelers** should rent **fuel-efficient 4x4 vehicles** and avoid unnecessary long drives.

**Limit Plastic Waste & Single-Use Items**

Bring a **reusable water bottle**—many lodges have **filtered water stations**.

Avoid buying **single-use plastic bottles, bags, or straws**.

**Respect Water Conservation Efforts**

Botswana and Namibia are **water-scarce regions**, so limit long showers and unnecessary water use.

Many eco-lodges use **bucket showers or water-efficient toilets** to reduce consumption.

### Choose Ethical & Low-Impact Activities

Prioritize **non-motorized activities** like **walking safaris, cycling tours, and kayaking** over carbon-heavy options.

Many national parks in Namibia offer **self-drive safaris**, reducing reliance on fuel-intensive tour vehicles.

## Volunteering & Giving Back

For travelers looking to go beyond sightseeing and make a difference, Botswana and Namibia offer numerous opportunities to volunteer in wildlife conservation, environmental restoration, and community development.

### Wildlife Conservation & Research Projects

### Cheetah Conservation Fund (Namibia)

Based near **Otjiwarongo, Namibia**, this globally recognized organization works to **protect endangered cheetahs through research, habitat restoration, and community education.**

Volunteers assist in **tracking cheetahs, collecting data, and maintaining conservation enclosures.**

### Okavango Wilderness Conservation (Botswana)

Supports **wetland preservation and wildlife monitoring in the Okavango Delta.**

Volunteers help with **research on elephant migration, anti-poaching efforts, and sustainable tourism development.**

### Naankuse Wildlife Sanctuary (Namibia)

Rescues and rehabilitates **injured and orphaned wildlife**, including leopards, baboons, and wild dogs.

Volunteers engage in **feeding, habitat maintenance, and environmental education projects.**

**Rhino Conservation at Khama Rhino Sanctuary (Botswana)**

A **community-led initiative protecting black and white rhinos.**

Volunteers can help with **tracking rhinos, patrolling for poachers, and assisting with conservation education programs.**

**Community-Based Volunteering**

**San Bushmen Cultural Preservation (Botswana & Namibia)**

Projects focus on **language preservation, traditional skills workshops, and education for San youth.**

Visitors can participate in **cultural exchange programs, storytelling sessions, and sustainable farming initiatives.**

**School & Literacy Programs**

Organizations like **Save the Rhino Trust (Namibia) and Elephants Without Borders (Botswana)** run **environmental education programs in local schools.**

Volunteers help teach **wildlife conservation, English, and sustainable agriculture.**

**Women's Empowerment Projects**

NGOs in Namibia and Botswana support **female artisans by promoting fair-trade crafts and business training.**

Visitors can contribute by purchasing handmade baskets, jewelry, and textiles directly from women's cooperatives.

# Chapter 11: 7-Day Combined Botswana & Namibia Itinerary

## Day 1: Arrival in Maun, Botswana & Okavango Delta Experience

### Morning

**Arrival in Maun**: Most tourists arrive at Maun International Airport (MUB), the gateway to the Okavango Delta. Flights from Johannesburg, Cape Town, or Windhoek typically arrive in the morning.

**Immigration & Transfers**: Upon landing, tourists complete immigration procedures and collect luggage.

**Breakfast**:

**Where to Eat**: The **Dusty Donkey Café** (affordable, relaxed setting), **Airport Junction Café** (convenient for travelers), or **Nokanyana Restaurant** (upscale option near the Thamalakane River).

**What to Eat**: Traditional Botswana breakfast—**fat cakes (magwinya)** with tea, scrambled eggs, or cereals for lighter options.

### Mid-Morning

**Scenic Flight Over the Okavango Delta**:

A **1-hour scenic flight** offers aerial views of the Delta's waterways and wildlife.

**Price**: $130–$200 per person (shared flight) or $600+ for a private charter.

**Getting Around**: Flights depart from **Maun Airport** via companies like Mack Air or Major Blue Air.

**Opening Hours**: Flights usually operate from **7 AM – 5 PM**.

### Afternoon

**Transfer to Okavango Delta Lodge**: Tourists travel to a safari lodge in the Okavango Delta by **motorboat or light aircraft** (depending on the lodge's location).

**Lunch:**

**Lodge Dining**: Meals typically include **grilled beef, pap (maize porridge), and fresh salads**.

**Alternative**: In Maun, tourists can have lunch at **The Red Monkey** (fusion cuisine) or **Old Bridge Backpackers** (casual riverside dining).

**Price**: $15–$35 per meal.

**Mid-Afternoon**

**Boat Safari on the Delta**: A guided **motorboat safari** allows tourists to see **hippos, crocodiles, elephants, and birdlife**.

**Price**: $100–$200 per person, included in some lodge packages.

**Duration**: 2–3 hours.

**Evening**

**Sunset at the Delta**: Tourists enjoy drinks while watching the sun set over the Delta's floodplains.

**Dinner:**

Lodge dinner includes **grilled game meat (kudu, ostrich), Botswana beef, vegetables, and desserts**.

**Where to Eat in Maun** (for those staying overnight):

**Thamalakane River Lodge** (upscale riverside dining, $20–$50 per meal).

**Tandurei Indian Restaurant** (Indian & local fusion, $10–$25 per meal).

**Night**

**Campfire & Stargazing**: Lodges offer storytelling around a **bonfire**, with guides sharing local myths.

**Overnight Stay**: Luxury lodges ($300–$1,500 per night) or budget camps ($80–$200 per night).

## Day 2: Mokoro Safari & Transfer to Moremi Game Reserve

**Morning**

**Sunrise Wildlife Viewing**: Early morning is the best time to see **big cats, wild dogs, and elephants.**

**Breakfast**:

Typical safari breakfast includes **fresh fruit, yogurt, pancakes, and coffee.**

Some lodges serve **biltong (dried meat), porridge, and eggs.**

**Mid-Morning**

**Mokoro Safari (Traditional Canoe Ride)**:

A **mokoro** (dugout canoe) safari through the **Delta's narrow channels.**

Best for spotting **kingfishers, antelopes, and frogs** up close.

**Price**: $50–$150 per person (included in some lodges).

**Duration**: 2–3 hours.

**Afternoon**

**Lunch at Lodge or Packed for Transfer**:

Typical options: **grilled chicken, rice, fresh salads, and fruit.**

**Transfer to Moremi Game Reserve**:

**Getting Around**: By **4x4 safari vehicle** (3–4 hours) or **charter flight** (30 minutes).

**Price**: $150–$500 per person (depending on the mode of transport).

**Entry Fees**:

Moremi Game Reserve entrance fee: **$12 per person.**

**Mid-Afternoon**

**First Game Drive in Moremi**: Tourists explore the diverse wildlife, including **lions, leopards, giraffes, and buffalos.**

### Evening

**Sundowner Safari Stop**: Drinks & snacks served while watching the sunset.

**Dinner at Safari Camp**:

**Menu**: Bush-style braai (barbecue), fresh fish, maize meal, and seasonal vegetables.

**Accommodation in Moremi**:

**Luxury Camps**: $500–$1,500 per night (e.g., Camp Xakanaxa, Khwai River Lodge).

**Mid-Range**: $250–$500 per night.

**Budget Camping**: $50–$150 per night.

### Night

**Night Safari Drive (Optional)**: Tourists can spot **nocturnal animals like leopards, hyenas, and owls**.

**Price**: $100–$300 per person (only allowed in certain private concessions).

# Day 3: Moremi Game Reserve to Savuti, Chobe National Park

**Morning**

**Early Game Drive in Moremi:**

Tourists embark on a **sunrise game drive (5:30 AM – 9:00 AM)** to spot **lions, leopards, elephants, and wild dogs.**

**Price**: $100–$200 per person (included in lodge packages).

**Getting Around**: Safari vehicles are provided by lodges, or tourists can self-drive in a **4x4 vehicle** (park fees: $30 per person + $10 per vehicle).

**Breakfast:**

**Lodge Breakfast**: Eggs, sausage, baked beans, toast, tea/coffee.

**Alternative**: If camping, travelers can have **oatmeal, fruit, or fat cakes (magwinya)** from local vendors.

**Mid-Morning**

**Transfer to Savuti, Chobe National Park:**

**Distance**: ~150 km (5–6 hours by 4x4).

**Route**: Drive through Khwai Community Area, spotting wildlife along the way.

**Getting Around**: Self-drive (4x4 essential) or transfer arranged by lodges.

**Afternoon**

**Arrival & Lunch in Savuti:**

Check into a **Savuti Safari Lodge** or **camping site**.

**Lunch Options:**

**Lodge Dining: Grilled chicken, vegetable stir-fry, and fresh salads.**

**Self-Drive Travelers**: Packed sandwiches or food from **Chobe Bush Camp.**

**Mid-Afternoon Game Drive:**

Explore **Savuti Marsh**, famous for large lion prides and elephant herds.

**Price**: $100–$250 per person for a guided safari.

**Evening**

**Sunset Safari & Photography Session**:

Capture **predators at dusk**.

Some lodges offer **sundowner drinks** in scenic spots.

**Dinner & Overnight Stay**:

**Dinner Options**:

Lodge dinner includes **beef stew, pap, and local vegetables**.

**Camping option**: Self-cooked meal or pre-packed meals.

**Where to Stay**:

**Luxury Lodges** ($500+ per night, all-inclusive).

**Mid-Range Camps** ($150–$300 per night).

**Budget Camping** ($50–$100 per night, self-catering).

# Day 4: Chobe River Safari & Transfer to Namibia (Caprivi Strip)

**Morning**

**Drive from Savuti to Chobe Riverfront** (~4 hours, 200 km).

**Breakfast** at the lodge or packed for the road: **fruit, muffins, tea/coffee**.

**Mid-Morning**

**Chobe River Safari (9 AM – 12 PM)**:

A **boat safari** along the Chobe River, spotting **hippos, crocodiles, elephants, and birdlife**.

**Price**: $50–$100 per person.

**Getting Around**: Depart from **Kasane** with a guided tour or self-arrange at **Chobe Marina Lodge**.

**Afternoon**

**Lunch in Kasane**:

**Places to Eat**:

**The Old House** (casual riverside dining, $15–$30 per meal).

**Chobe Safari Lodge Restaurant** (buffet-style, $20–$40 per meal).

**Transfer to Namibia's Caprivi Strip (Zambezi Region)**:

**Border Crossing**: Kazungula Border Post (~1 hour).

**Getting Around**: Self-drive or arranged transfer (~3 hours to Kongola).

**Visa Fees**: Some nationalities pay ~$30 for a Namibian visa.

**Mid-Afternoon**

**Arrival & Check-in at a Lodge** in Caprivi Strip.

**Relaxation by the River** or a **short sunset boat cruise** ($40–$80 per person).

**Evening & Night**

**Dinner at Lodge**: Fresh fish (tilapia), grilled meats, and local vegetables.

**Overnight Stay**: Luxury lodges ($250+), mid-range options ($100–$200), or budget campsites ($50).

# Day 5: Drive to Etosha National Park, Namibia

**Morning**

**Breakfast in Caprivi Strip** (Zambezi Region, Namibia):

**Where to Eat:**

**Caprivi Houseboat Safari Lodge** (riverfront breakfast, $10–$20 per meal).

**Zambezi Mubala Lodge** (buffet-style breakfast, $15–$25).

**What to Eat**: Eggs, bacon, fresh fruit, homemade bread, and Namibian **vetkoek (fried dough)**.

**Drive from Caprivi Strip to Etosha National Park** (~8–9 hours, 700 km):

**Route**:

Drive west via Rundu, Grootfontein, and Tsumeb.

Stops for fuel/snacks in **Rundu and Tsumeb**.

**Getting Around**:

Self-drive in a **4x4 rental** ($80–$150 per day).

Private guided transfers ($250–$400 per vehicle).

**Mid-Morning & Afternoon**

**Lunch Stop in Tsumeb (Optional)**:

**Where to Eat:**

**Kupferquelle Resort Restaurant** (international & local cuisine, $15–$25 per meal).

**Etosha Café** (affordable, quick meals, $10–$20).

**What to Eat**: Beef fillet, fresh salads, chicken schnitzel, or a veggie platter.

**Arrival at Etosha National Park (~3 PM–4 PM)**:

Check-in at lodges/campsites inside or near the park.

**Entrance Fee**: $7 per person + $10 per vehicle.

**Opening Hours: Sunrise to Sunset** (varies by season).

**Mid-Afternoon**

**Short Game Drive in Etosha:**

**Where to Visit:**

**Okaukuejo Waterhole** (great for elephant & rhino sightings).

**Namutoni Area** (lion & cheetah hotspots).

**Price:** Included in park entry for self-drive; $50–$100 per person for guided safaris.

**Evening & Night**

**Dinner & Overnight Stay:**

**Where to Eat:**

**Etosha Safari Lodge Restaurant** (buffet-style, $20–$40 per meal).

**Mokuti Lodge Restaurant** (fine dining, $25–$50 per meal).

**What to Eat:** Namibian **braai (grilled meat), vegetable stew, and mieliepap (maize porridge)**.

**Overnight Options:**

**Luxury Lodges** ($300–$700 per night).

**Mid-Range Lodges** ($150–$250 per night).

**Camping Sites** ($30–$80 per night).

## Day 6: Etosha Safari & Transfer to Swakopmund

**Morning**

**Sunrise Game Drive (6 AM – 9 AM):**

**Best Areas:**

**Halali Waterhole** (good for big cats).

**Etosha Pan** (unique salt pan landscape).

**Price**: Self-drive (park fee only) or $50–$150 per person for guided tours.

**Breakfast at the Lodge:**

**What to Eat**: Omelet, toast, fruit, yogurt, and Namibian coffee.

**Mid-Morning**

**Drive from Etosha to Swakopmund (~6–7 hours, 500 km):**

**Route:**

Via Outjo and Karibib.

Stops in **Outjo (bakery stop)** and Usakos (fuel/snacks).

**Getting Around:**

Self-drive (4x4 recommended).

Private transfers (~$250–$400 per vehicle).

**Afternoon**

**Lunch Stop in Omaruru** (Optional):

**Where to Eat:**

**Kashana Restaurant** (international cuisine, $15–$30 per meal).

**Omaruru Guesthouse Café** (light meals, $10–$20).

**What to Eat**: Game steak, fresh salads, or chicken wraps.

**Mid-Afternoon**

**Arrival in Swakopmund (~3 PM–4 PM):**

Check-in at hotels or guesthouses.

Rest or explore the town's **German colonial architecture**.

**Evening**

**Sunset Walk on Swakopmund Beach.**

**Dinner in Swakopmund:**

**Where to Eat:**

**The Tug Restaurant** (seafood, ocean views, $25–$50 per meal).

**Jetty 1905** (grilled fish, cocktails, $20–$45 per meal).

**What to Eat: Namibian kingklip fish, oysters, or game meat steaks.**

**Night**

**Overnight in Swakopmund:**

**Luxury Hotels** ($250–$500 per night).

**Mid-Range Hotels** ($100–$200 per night).

**Budget Guesthouses** ($40–$80 per night).

## Day 7: Sossusvlei Dunes & Departure from Windhoek

**Morning**

**Drive from Swakopmund to Sossusvlei** *(~5 hours, 350 km)*

**Getting Around**:

Self-drive (4x4 recommended, road is rough).

Tour transfers ($100–$150 per person).

**Breakfast on the Go**:

**Pack croissants, fruit, and coffee** from Swakopmund bakeries.

**Sossusvlei & Deadvlei Visit (6:00 AM – 10:00 AM)**

**Entry Fee**: N$150 ($8) per person.

**Hike Big Daddy Dune (325m high)** for stunning views.

**Visit Deadvlei** for unique dried-up acacia trees.

**Mid-Morning**

**Sesriem Canyon Walk (10:30 AM – 11:30 AM)**

**Short 1-hour hike** to explore 30m-deep rock formations.

**Free entry** with Sossusvlei permit.

**Afternoon**

**Drive to Windhoek (~4.5 hours, 360 km)**.

Stop at **Solitaire Bakery** for **apple pie** and refreshments.

**Lunch Options**:

**Jojos in Windhoek** (casual burgers & wraps).

**The Stellenbosch Wine Bar** (steak & seafood).

**Price Range**: N$150–N$350 ($8–$20) per meal.

**Mid-Afternoon**

**Explore Windhoek Before Departure**:

**Craft Market** for souvenirs (open until 5 PM).

**Christuskirche & Independence Museum** (free entry, open until 5 PM).

**Evening & Departure**

**Early Dinner in Windhoek**:

**Where to Eat**:

**Joe's Beerhouse** (traditional game meat).

**Sardinia Blue Olive** (Italian cuisine).

**What to Eat: Springbok steak, venison platter, or grilled fish.**

**Price Range**: N$250–N$500 ($15–$30).

**Airport Transfer to Hosea Kutako International Airport (WDH)**

Taxis or shuttle ($15–$30).

Flight Check-in (2–3 hours before departure).

**Night**

**Departure Flight from Windhoek** *(Most flights to Johannesburg, Frankfurt, or Cape Town depart at night).*

# Chapter 12: Travel Tips & Practical Information

## Language & Communication

**Official & Widely Spoken Languages**

**Botswana**

**English** – The official language, used in government, education, and business.

**Setswana (Tswana)** – The most widely spoken indigenous language, understood by nearly 80% of the population.

Other languages: **Kalanga, Sekgalagadi, and San languages** spoken in different regions.

**Namibia**

**English** – The official language, though not the most commonly spoken at home.

**Oshiwambo** – The most widely spoken indigenous language, mainly in the northern regions.

**Afrikaans** – Historically a dominant language, still widely used in business and everyday conversations.

**German** – Spoken by some communities, particularly in Windhoek and Swakopmund.

Other languages: **Herero, Nama/Damara, and San languages** spoken in different parts of the country.

**Basic Phrases to Know**

While English is widely spoken, learning a few local words can enhance cultural interactions:

**Hello** – **Dumela** (Botswana – Setswana), **Hallo** (Namibia – Afrikaans)

**Thank you** – **Ke a leboga** (Botswana – Setswana), **Dankie** (Namibia – Afrikaans)

**Yes/No** – **Ee / Nnyaa** (Botswana – Setswana), **Ja / Nee** (Namibia – Afrikaans)

**How are you?** – **O tsogile jang?** (Botswana – Setswana), **Hoe gaan dit?** (Namibia – Afrikaans)

**Goodbye** – **Sala Sentle** (Botswana – Setswana), **Totsiens** (Namibia – Afrikaans)

### Cultural Communication Tips

**Respect for elders** – In both Botswana and Namibia, addressing elders with courtesy is expected.

**Handshakes** – A common greeting, sometimes accompanied by a slight bow or nod.

**Directness in conversation** – Namibians tend to be more direct, while Batswana often use indirect speech to maintain politeness.

**Avoid rushing conversations** – Small talk is valued before discussing business matters.

## Currency & Payment Options

### Currencies Used

**Botswana – Botswana Pula (BWP)**

1 Pula = 100 Thebe

Widely accepted in shops, hotels, and restaurants.

**Namibia – Namibian Dollar (NAD)**

1 Namibian Dollar = 100 Cents

**South African Rand (ZAR) is also legal tender in Namibia** and can be used interchangeably with NAD.

### Cash vs. Card Payments

**Cash** – Recommended for small towns, markets, and rural areas where card payments may not be available.

**Credit & Debit Cards** – Widely accepted in **hotels, restaurants, and major retail stores**. Visa and Mastercard are the most commonly used; American Express and Diners Club may have limited acceptance.

**ATMs** – Available in major cities and towns but may have withdrawal limits for international cards.

### Mobile & Digital Payments

**Botswana** – Mobile payment platforms like **Orange Money and Mascom MyZaka** are popular for local transactions.

**Namibia** – **eWallet (FNB Namibia) and PayToday** allow for quick mobile payments.

### Currency Exchange & Tipping

**Exchange money at banks or licensed forex bureaus** rather than airports, which often have higher fees.

**Tipping** – 10-15% in restaurants is customary; safari guides and lodge staff typically receive **USD 5–10 per day** in tips.

## Electricity & Internet Connectivity

### Power Supply & Electrical Outlets

**Voltage**: Both Botswana and Namibia operate on **220–240V, 50Hz**.

**Plug Type**: The most common plug types are Type M (three large round pins) and Type D (three smaller round pins).

**Power Availability**:

In major cities like Gaborone, Windhoek, Maun, and Swakopmund, electricity is reliable, with occasional outages.

In remote safari lodges, rural villages, and conservation areas, power is often generated by solar energy, diesel generators, or a combination of both. Some eco-lodges rely entirely on solar power, and guests may need to limit their electricity use, especially for charging electronics.

### Internet & Mobile Connectivity

**Urban Areas**: Fast and reliable 4G mobile networks and Wi-Fi are available in hotels, cafés, airports, and business centers in cities like Gaborone, Maun, Windhoek, and Swakopmund.

**Safari Camps & Remote Areas**: Internet access is often limited or nonexistent in wildlife reserves, national parks, and desert regions. Some high-end lodges offer Wi-Fi in common areas, but speeds may be slow.

**Mobile Networks**:

**Botswana**: Mascom, Orange, and BTC Mobile provide the best coverage.

**Namibia**: MTC and Telecom Namibia are the leading providers.

Travelers should buy a **local SIM card** for affordable data and calls.

**Satellite Internet**: Some remote lodges use satellite connections, but speeds can be slow, and usage may be restricted.

## Tipping & Local Etiquette

**Tipping Culture in Botswana & Namibia**

Tipping is **not mandatory** but is generally appreciated, especially in tourism-related services.

**General Tipping Guidelines**

**Restaurants & Cafés**: 10–15% of the bill if service is not included.

**Safari Guides & Trackers**:

Guides: **$10–$20 per person per day** (shared among guides and trackers).

Trackers & Spotters: **$5–$10 per day**.

Lodge Staff: **$5–$10 per stay** in a communal tip box.

**Hotel Staff**:

Housekeeping: **$2–$5 per day**.

Porters: **$1–$2 per bag**.

**Taxi Drivers**: Rounding up the fare is sufficient.

## Local Etiquette & Social Norms

**Greetings Matter** – In both countries, greeting someone before starting a conversation is important. A handshake is common, sometimes with a slight nod or bow.

**Respect for Elders** – Address elders with courtesy and wait for them to initiate greetings.

**Dress Code** – While casual wear is acceptable, modest dressing is preferred in rural areas and traditional communities.

**Photography** – Always ask permission before taking photos of people, especially in indigenous communities.

**Punctuality** – While business settings follow Western punctuality, social events and casual meetings may operate on **"African time,"** meaning they could start later than scheduled.

# Emergency Contacts & Useful Numbers

## Botswana

### General Emergency Numbers

**Police:** 999

**Ambulance:** 997

**Fire Department:** 998

### Medical Assistance

**Private Ambulance Services (Gaborone & Major Cities):**

**Bokamoso Private Hospital:** +267 369 4000

**Gaborone Private Hospital:** +267 368 5600

**AEMS (Ambulance Emergency Medical Services):** +267 390 3030

### Roadside Assistance

**Botswana Automobile Association (BAA):** +267 391 3295

**Toll-Free Emergency Roadside Help:** 0800 600 233

### Tourist Assistance

**Tourism Emergency Hotline (Botswana Tourism Organisation):** +267 391 3111

**Embassies & Consulates:** Contact your country's diplomatic mission in Gaborone for consular assistance.

## Namibia

### General Emergency Numbers

**Police:** 10111

**Ambulance:** 211 111 (Windhoek) / 081 924 (Nationwide)

**Fire Department:** 211 111

**Medical Assistance**

**Private Ambulance Services (Windhoek & Major Cities):**

**E-Med Rescue 24:** +264 61 411 600

**MedRescue Namibia:** +264 83 331 1246

**Mediclinic Windhoek:** +264 61 222 687

**Roadside Assistance**

**Automobile Association of Namibia (AAN):** +264 61 224 201

**Toll-Free Emergency Roadside Help:** 081 924

**Tourist Assistance**

**Tourist Police (Windhoek):** +264 61 209 4345

**Namibia Tourism Board (for travel-related issues):** +264 61 290 6000

**Embassies & Consulates:** Located mainly in Windhoek; contact for consular support if needed.

**Additional Tips**

When traveling to remote areas, inform your lodge or guide about your itinerary.

Carry a **satellite phone or emergency GPS beacon** in desert or wilderness regions where mobile networks may be unavailable.

Save emergency contacts on your phone and keep a printed copy in case of battery failure.

# Chapter 13: Frequently Asked Questions (FAQs)

## Common Traveler Concerns Answered

### Is Botswana and Namibia Safe for Tourists?

Both countries are considered **safe for tourists**, with relatively low crime rates compared to other African destinations. However, travelers should still take precautions:

**Petty crime (pickpocketing and bag snatching)** can occur in cities like Gaborone and Windhoek. Avoid displaying valuables in public.

**Avoid walking alone at night**, especially in urban areas. Use registered taxis or hotel transport.

**Wildlife encounters** are a risk in national parks. Always follow your guide's instructions and avoid getting too close to animals.

**Road safety** is a concern, especially for self-drivers. Be cautious of wildlife and unpaved roads in rural areas.

### What Health Precautions Should I Take?

**Malaria:** Botswana's Okavango Delta and northern Namibia (Caprivi Strip) are malaria-risk areas. Take anti-malarial medication and use insect repellent.

**Vaccinations:** Routine vaccinations (Hepatitis A, Hepatitis B, Typhoid, and Tetanus) are recommended. A **yellow fever vaccine** is required if arriving from a yellow fever-endemic country.

**Water Safety:** Tap water in major cities is safe to drink, but in remote areas, use bottled or purified water.

**Medical Facilities:** Private hospitals in Windhoek and Gaborone are well-equipped. Remote areas have limited medical services, so **travel insurance with emergency evacuation coverage is recommended.**

### How Do I Get Around?

**Domestic Flights:** Small charter flights operate between safari lodges in Botswana and Namibia.

**Self-Drive:** Namibia is a great self-drive destination with well-maintained roads, while Botswana requires **4x4 vehicles** for off-road terrain.

**Public Transport:** Minibuses and shared taxis are available in cities but are not recommended for long-distance travel.

**Guided Tours:** Many visitors prefer joining guided safaris to explore remote areas safely and conveniently.

### What Currency is Accepted?

Botswana uses the **Pula (BWP)**, and Namibia uses the **Namibian Dollar (NAD)**. The **South African Rand (ZAR)** is also accepted in Namibia.

Credit cards are widely accepted in hotels, lodges, and restaurants but **cash is needed for rural areas, markets, and small businesses**.

ATMs are available in cities, but it's advisable to carry some cash for remote areas.

### What Should I Pack?

**Lightweight, breathable clothing** for warm days and **a jacket** for cool desert nights.

**Neutral-colored clothing** for safaris (avoid bright colors that can scare animals).

**A good pair of walking shoes or hiking boots** for exploring.

**Binoculars and a camera** for wildlife viewing.

**Power adapter (Type M or D plugs)** for charging electronics.

### What Cultural Norms Should I Be Aware Of?

Greetings are important. A handshake or a polite "hello" is expected before starting a conversation.

Dress modestly when visiting rural villages or religious sites.

Always ask permission before taking photos of people, especially indigenous communities like the San Bushmen or Himba.

Respect wildlife and avoid littering in national parks.

### Is Internet and Mobile Connectivity Reliable?

Internet and mobile networks are strong in cities but **limited in remote safari areas**.

Purchasing a **local SIM card** (Mascom, Orange in Botswana; MTC in Namibia) is recommended for data and calls.

Many lodges offer **Wi-Fi, but speeds may be slow** in the wilderness.

### What's the Best Time to Visit?

**Dry season (May to October):** Best for wildlife viewing as animals gather around water sources. Cool mornings, warm afternoons, and little rainfall.

**Green season (November to April):** Lush landscapes, fewer crowds, and great birdwatching, but some roads may be difficult to navigate due to rains.

# Safety Tips for Solo Travelers

## General Safety Tips

**Stay informed**: Research local customs, weather conditions, and political updates before traveling.

**Register with your embassy**: Many embassies offer registration services for travelers in case of emergencies.

**Keep emergency contacts handy**: Save local police, medical assistance, and your country's embassy contacts.

**Avoid carrying large sums of cash**: Use credit/debit cards where possible, and withdraw cash only from ATMs in secure locations.

**Trust your instincts**: If a situation feels unsafe, remove yourself from it immediately.

## Accommodation Safety

Choose well-reviewed hotels, lodges, or guesthouses with **good security measures**.

Inform the hotel staff of your **daily plans and expected return time**.

Lock your doors and windows at night, even in safari lodges.

Avoid ground-floor rooms where security may be lower.

## Transportation Safety

**Self-driving**:

In Namibia, road conditions can be challenging, especially in the desert. Stick to **main roads** and ensure your vehicle is in **good condition** with enough fuel.

In Botswana, a **4x4 is essential** for off-road conditions. Wildlife crossings and deep sand can make driving difficult.

**Taxis & Ridesharing**:

Always use **registered taxis** or arrange transport through hotels.

Avoid accepting rides from strangers.

**Public Transport:**

Buses and shared taxis are common but may not follow set schedules. Keep an eye on your belongings.

### Outdoor & Wildlife Safety

**Never hike alone** in remote areas—join a guided tour or group.

**Stick to marked trails** in national parks and game reserves.

**Follow safari guide instructions**—wild animals can be unpredictable.

**Carry a fully charged phone, map, and enough water** when exploring.

**Be cautious of extreme weather**—the desert can be very hot during the day and cold at night.

### Social & Cultural Safety

Respect **local customs and dress modestly** in villages or religious sites.

Avoid discussing **politics or controversial topics** with strangers.

Be mindful when interacting with **locals offering help**—most are friendly, but scams exist in tourist areas.

If **harassed or feeling unsafe**, move to a public space and seek assistance from authorities or hotel staff.

### Staying Connected & Emergency Preparedness

**Buy a local SIM card** for reliable mobile data access.

**Share your itinerary** with a trusted person, updating them regularly.

**Have travel insurance** covering medical emergencies and evacuation.

**Carry a whistle, flashlight, and small first-aid kit** for emergencies.

# Family-Friendly Travel Advice

## Best Time to Visit

**Dry season (May to October)** is ideal for wildlife viewing, as animals gather around water sources.

**Green season (November to April)** has lush landscapes and fewer crowds but higher temperatures and occasional rain.

**For families with young children**, the cooler months (May to August) are more comfortable.

## Choosing Family-Friendly Accommodations

Look for **lodges and camps** that welcome children and offer **family suites, child-friendly meals, and kid-focused activities.**

Many **high-end lodges** have **minimum age restrictions** for game drives, so check before booking.

Consider **self-catering lodges** or accommodations with a **pool and play areas**.

**Eco-lodges and farm stays** in Namibia provide a fun, educational experience.

## Wildlife Safaris with Kids

**Private game drives** offer more flexibility for families than group tours.

Some lodges offer **child-friendly game drives** with shorter durations and interactive guides.

**Keep kids engaged** with binoculars, wildlife checklists, and animal tracking lessons.

**Ensure children follow safety rules**—never leave the vehicle and always listen to guides.

## Outdoor Adventures for Families

**Boat Safaris**: Chobe River in Botswana and the Okavango Delta offer safe, relaxing boat rides for families.

**Sand Dune Adventures**: Kids love climbing the **Sossusvlei dunes** in Namibia and sliding down the sand.

**Cultural Visits**: Meet **San Bushmen in Botswana** or **Himba communities in Namibia** for hands-on learning.

**Kayaking in Walvis Bay**: See playful seals and dolphins up close in a safe environment.

### Food & Dining for Families

Most hotels and lodges offer **child-friendly menus** with simple, familiar meals.

In cities, family-friendly restaurants serve **grilled meats, fresh seafood, and vegetarian options**.

**Pack snacks and bottled water** for road trips and long game drives.

### Health & Safety Tips

**Vaccinations & Malaria Precautions**: If traveling to **malaria-risk areas (Okavango Delta, Caprivi Strip)**, consult a doctor about **anti-malarial medication**.

**Sun Protection**: High SPF sunscreen, wide-brim hats, and light, long-sleeved clothing are essential.

**Car Seats & Travel Gear**: Bring a **car seat** if planning a self-drive trip, as they are not always available for rent.

**Emergency Contacts**: Save local emergency numbers and ensure you have travel insurance covering medical care.

### Keeping Kids Entertained During Travel

**Long drives** are common in Namibia and Botswana, so bring **games, audiobooks, and activity books**.

**Wildlife spotting games** keep kids engaged on game drives.

**Storytelling about local myths and animals** can make the trip more immersive.

# Best Times to Visit Specific Regions

**Botswana**

**Okavango Delta (Best: May–October)**

**Why?** The dry season brings low water levels in surrounding areas, forcing wildlife to congregate around permanent water sources.

**Highlights:** Peak wildlife viewing, excellent boat safaris and mokoro (canoe) trips through flooded plains.

**Low Season (November–April):** Lush landscapes and fewer crowds, but higher temperatures and occasional rain.

**Chobe National Park (Best: May–October)**

**Why?** Large concentrations of elephants and other animals gather along the **Chobe River** during the dry season.

**Highlights: Boat safaris**, predator sightings, and dramatic animal interactions at watering holes.

**Low Season (November–April):** Greener landscapes with **baby animals** but harder-to-spot wildlife.

**Makgadikgadi Pans & Nxai Pan (Best: November–April)**

**Why?** This is the **wet season**, when the salt pans transform into a wildlife-rich wetland.

**Highlights:** Flamingo migrations, zebra herds, and dramatic thunderstorms over the vast plains.

**Dry Season (May–October):** Unique **desert landscapes and quad biking**, but less wildlife.

**Central Kalahari Game Reserve (Best: December–April)**

**Why?** Summer rains bring **lush vegetation and abundant prey**, attracting **big cats like lions and cheetahs**.

**Highlights:** The **green season safari experience** with excellent predator sightings.

**Dry Season (May–November):** Harsh conditions but great for **desert-adapted wildlife**.

### Namibia

### Etosha National Park (Best: May–October)

**Why?** The dry season forces wildlife to **gather around Etosha's waterholes**, making them easy to spot.

**Highlights:** Large herds of elephants, lions, and rare **black rhinos** at key waterholes.

**Low Season (November–April):** Lush landscapes with newborn animals, but wildlife is more dispersed.

### Sossusvlei & Namib Desert (Best: April–October)

**Why?** Cooler temperatures make exploring the dunes more comfortable.

**Highlights:** Climbing **Big Daddy or Dune 45**, visiting **Deadvlei**, and stunning sunrises over the desert.

**Low Season (November–March):** Very hot daytime temperatures can make hiking difficult.

### Skeleton Coast & Swakopmund (Best: September–April)

**Why?** Warmer temperatures make **coastal activities like kayaking, dolphin watching, and sandboarding** more pleasant.

**Highlights:** Cape fur seals at **Cape Cross**, shipwreck photography, and adventure sports.

**Low Season (May–August):** Cold Atlantic winds and foggy mornings, but fewer crowds.

### Damaraland (Best: May–October)

**Why?** The dry season makes spotting **desert-adapted elephants and black rhinos** easier.

**Highlights:** Twyfelfontein rock engravings, Petrified Forest, and remote landscapes.

**Low Season (November–April):** Occasional rain, but landscapes turn green with seasonal rivers and waterfalls.

### Caprivi Strip (Zambezi Region) (Best: May–September)

**Why?** This is Namibia's most **tropical region**, best visited in the **cooler dry season** for game viewing.

**Highlights:** River safaris, excellent birdwatching, and wildlife-rich reserves like **Bwabwata National Park**.

**Low Season (October–April):** Rainy and humid, but lush scenery with peak birdwatching.

## Travel Hacks & Money-Saving Tips

**Money-Saving Tips**

**Travel During Shoulder or Low Season**

Peak season (June–October) is the most expensive for safaris and accommodations. Instead, visit during the shoulder season (April–May, November) for better deals and fewer crowds. In Namibia, the green season (November–April) offers discounted rates while still providing excellent wildlife sightings.

**Book Flights & Accommodations in Advance**

Flights to Botswana and Namibia can be pricey. Booking at least 3–6 months in advance helps secure the best rates. Many safari lodges and camps offer early booking discounts or special packages.

**Consider Self-Drive Safaris**

Guided safaris can be expensive, but Namibia and some parts of Botswana (excluding the Okavango Delta) are excellent for self-drive trips. Renting a 4x4 with rooftop camping allows you to save on accommodation costs and explore at your own pace.

**Use Budget-Friendly Accommodations**

Campsites and self-catering lodges are significantly cheaper than luxury safari lodges. Namibia has excellent government-run rest camps in Etosha and other parks. In Botswana, community-run campsites offer a more affordable and immersive experience.

### Travel in a Group

Costs for car rentals, fuel, and accommodations drop significantly when shared. Some lodges offer group discounts, making it more affordable to split expenses.

### Eat Local & Shop Smart

Restaurants in major cities can be pricey. Opting for local markets and food stalls provides traditional meals at a fraction of the cost. Buying snacks and drinks at supermarkets before heading into remote areas helps avoid inflated safari lodge prices.

### Choose Budget-Friendly Safari Options

Public game parks like Etosha, Chobe, and Moremi are more affordable than private reserves while still offering great wildlife viewing. Instead of expensive fly-in safaris, overland tours or mobile safaris provide a cheaper and adventurous experience.

### Avoid Pricey Currency Exchange Fees

Withdrawing cash from ATMs is cheaper than exchanging money at airports or hotels, which have higher fees. Using credit cards with no foreign transaction fees saves on exchange rate markups.

### Use Public Transport Where Possible

In cities like Windhoek and Gaborone, taxis and buses are more affordable than renting a car for short distances. For long-distance travel in Namibia, the Intercape Bus is a budget-friendly alternative to domestic flights.

### Pack Smart to Avoid Extra Costs

Bringing a reusable water bottle and water purification tablets reduces the need to buy bottled water. Packing binoculars and camera gear instead of renting at lodges saves money. Carrying basic medical supplies helps avoid overpriced medications at tourist locations.

# Chapter 14: Conclusion
## Final Travel Tips & Recommendations

**Packing Essentials**

**Light, breathable clothing** for hot days and **warm layers** for cool mornings and evenings, especially in the desert.

**Comfortable walking shoes** for safaris, hikes, and exploring towns.

**Sun protection**, including a hat, sunglasses, and high-SPF sunscreen.

**Binoculars** for wildlife spotting and a **good camera** for capturing the scenery.

**Reusable water bottle** with a filter to stay hydrated while reducing plastic waste.

**Basic first aid kit** with any necessary medications, insect repellent, and motion sickness pills for long drives.

**Health & Safety Tips**

**Malaria precautions**: If traveling to malaria-prone areas like the Okavango Delta or Caprivi Strip, take anti-malarial medication and use insect repellent.

**Stay hydrated**, especially in the desert regions where heat exhaustion is a risk.

**Follow wildlife safety guidelines**: Keep a safe distance from animals, never feed them, and always listen to guides.

**Emergency contacts**: Save local emergency numbers, embassy details, and medical assistance contacts.

**Transportation Tips**

**Self-driving** is a great way to explore Namibia but requires a 4x4 for remote areas and gravel roads. Always carry extra fuel, water, and a spare tire.

**Botswana's safari parks** have deep sand and water crossings, so hiring a driver or joining a guided tour may be better for those unfamiliar with off-road driving.

**Public transport is limited**, so plan intercity travel in advance, especially in Namibia, where distances between destinations are long.

### Cultural Etiquette

**Greet locals respectfully** and learn a few basic phrases in Setswana or Oshiwambo to show appreciation.

**Respect cultural traditions**, especially when visiting indigenous communities like the San Bushmen and Himba people. Ask before taking photos.

**Tipping** is expected in restaurants (10%–15%) and for guides, drivers, and hotel staff.

### Money-Saving Strategies

**Withdraw cash** from ATMs in major towns instead of exchanging money at airports.

**Book accommodations and tours in advance** to secure lower prices.

**Eat at local markets** and self-cater when possible to save on food costs.

### Best Travel Apps & Resources

**Maps.me or Google Maps** for offline navigation.

**iOverlander** for self-drive travelers looking for campsites, fuel stations, and road conditions.

**XE Currency** to track exchange rates and avoid overpaying.

**Park apps and tourism websites** for real-time updates on wildlife sightings and road closures.

## Reflecting on Your Botswana & Namibia Journey

A journey through Botswana and Namibia is more than just an adventure—it is an immersion into vast landscapes, thriving wildlife, and rich cultural heritage. Whether you explored the Okavango Delta, stood atop the towering dunes of Sossusvlei, or connected with local communities, your experiences leave lasting impressions.

Take time to reflect on:

**Memorable moments**: What stood out the most? Was it a thrilling game drive, a breathtaking sunset over the Namib Desert, or a conversation with a local artisan?

**Personal growth**: How has this journey changed your perspective on nature, conservation, or different ways of life?

**Lessons learned**: Traveling through remote areas teaches resilience, adaptability, and the value of respecting the environment.

Sharing your experiences through storytelling, photography, or journaling not only preserves memories but also inspires others to explore Botswana and Namibia responsibly.

## Encouraging Sustainable Travel Practices

As two of Africa's most ecologically sensitive destinations, Botswana and Namibia thrive on conservation efforts. By traveling sustainably, visitors can help protect these incredible landscapes and cultures for future generations.

**Responsible Wildlife Tourism**

**Choose ethical safari operators** that support conservation and avoid those offering hands-on animal encounters.

**Observe wildlife from a distance** to minimize stress on animals and follow park regulations.

**Avoid purchasing animal products** such as ivory, skins, or anything derived from endangered species.

**Supporting Local Communities**

**Stay at eco-lodges** that contribute to conservation and employ locals.

**Shop responsibly** by purchasing handmade crafts from community-run markets rather than mass-produced souvenirs.

**Respect cultural traditions** and seek out authentic experiences, such as guided visits with the San Bushmen or Himba people.

**Minimizing Environmental Impact**

**Reduce plastic waste** by carrying a reusable water bottle and eco-friendly toiletries.

**Use water and electricity sparingly**, especially in desert regions where resources are limited.

**Stick to marked trails** while hiking or driving to protect fragile ecosystems.

## How to Stay Connected with Fellow Travelers

Traveling through Botswana and Namibia can be a deeply immersive experience, but given the vast landscapes and remote locations, staying connected with fellow travelers can enhance your journey. Whether you are looking for companionship, travel advice, or a sense of community while on the road, there are several ways to build and maintain connections.

**Online Travel Communities & Forums**

Before and during your trip, engaging with online travel communities can be invaluable for advice, trip planning, and meeting like-minded adventurers. Some useful platforms include:

**Facebook groups** such as "Backpacking Africa" and "Traveling Namibia & Botswana" provide insights from fellow travelers.

**Reddit travel forums**, like r/travel and r/AfricaTravel, are great for discussing routes, visa requirements, and local tips.

**iOverlander**, a mobile app that helps overlanders and campers share information on road conditions, campsites, and fuel stations.

**Couchsurfing Hangouts**, a feature of Couchsurfing, allows travelers to meet for meals or activities in real-time.

**Travel Apps for Real-Time Communication**

**WhatsApp and Telegram**: Most locals and fellow travelers use these for messaging, and they work well even with limited internet connectivity.

**Zello**: A walkie-talkie-style app that can be used in remote areas where cellular networks are weak.

**Nomad List**: Helps digital nomads and long-term travelers connect in specific destinations.

### Meeting People at Hostels, Campsites & Lodges

Botswana and Namibia have excellent hostels, guesthouses, and lodges that encourage social interaction.

**Hostels and backpacker lodges** in places like Windhoek, Swakopmund, and Maun offer communal kitchens, group tours, and shared dorms, making it easy to meet people.

**Campsites in national parks and remote areas** often have shared facilities where travelers exchange stories and travel tips.

**Overland safari tours** provide built-in communities, as groups travel together in customized trucks for multi-day adventures.

### Joining Group Activities & Experiences

Participating in group excursions is an easy way to meet fellow travelers. Some options include:

**Guided safaris** in Chobe, Moremi, and Etosha National Parks.

**Kayaking tours** in Walvis Bay, where small groups explore the coastline together.

**Cultural experiences**, such as visiting the San Bushmen or Himba communities, often involve multiple travelers.

**Multi-day treks** like the Fish River Canyon hike in Namibia, where hikers naturally bond over the journey.

### Volunteer & Work Exchange Programs

Joining conservation or community projects can connect you with like-minded people while making a positive impact.

**Wildlife conservation programs** in the Okavango Delta, where volunteers assist with research and eco-tourism.

**Farm stays and eco-lodges** that offer work exchange programs in exchange for accommodation.

**Teaching or community outreach projects** in rural villages, where travelers contribute their skills while experiencing local life.

Staying connected with fellow travelers enhances the journey, provides safety in numbers, and creates lasting friendships. By using a mix of digital tools and in-person interactions, visitors to Botswana and Namibia can enjoy a more enriching travel experience.

## Resources for Further Exploration

Botswana and Namibia are vast countries with incredible landscapes, wildlife, and cultural experiences. To continue learning and planning beyond your initial trip, here are key resources that offer in-depth insights and practical guidance.

### Books & Travel Guides

*Bradt Travel Guide: Namibia* – A detailed guide covering the country's attractions, history, and travel tips.

*Bradt Travel Guide: Botswana & The Okavango Delta* – A must-read for wildlife enthusiasts, offering expert advice on safaris.

*The Safari Companion* by Richard D. Estes – A great resource for understanding animal behavior during game drives.

*Cry of the Kalahari* by Mark and Delia Owens – A fascinating true story about wildlife research in Botswana.

### Official Tourism Websites

**Botswana Tourism Board** (www.botswanatourism.co.bw) – Offers up-to-date information on parks, accommodations, and travel tips.

**Namibia Tourism Board** (www.namibiatourism.com.na) – Covers destinations, visa requirements, and suggested itineraries.

### Maps & Navigation Apps

**Tracks4Africa** – The best GPS map for self-drive safaris, with detailed road conditions, campsites, and fuel stops.

**Google Maps & Maps.me** – Useful for urban areas and offline navigation in remote locations.

## Wildlife & Conservation Organizations

**Kavango-Zambezi Transfrontier Conservation Area (KAZA)** – A regional conservation effort linking Botswana, Namibia, Zimbabwe, Zambia, and Angola.

**Okavango Wilderness Project** – Focuses on preserving the Okavango Delta's fragile ecosystem.

**Save the Rhino Trust Namibia** – Works on protecting endangered rhinos in Namibia's deserts.

## Local Blogs & YouTube Channels

**Travel blogs like Expert Vagabond, The Blonde Abroad, and We Are Africa** provide firsthand travel experiences and updated insights.

**YouTube channels such as WildEarth and SafariLIVE** stream live game drives from Botswana's reserves.

## Safari & Adventure Booking Platforms

**SafariBookings.com** – Compares different safari packages in Botswana and Namibia.

**GetYourGuide & Viator** – Offers tours, activities, and day trips with reviews from past travelers.

## Conservation & Sustainable Travel Resources

**Responsible Travel** – A platform that connects travelers with ethical tourism operators.

**The Long Run** – Lists eco-lodges committed to sustainability and conservation in Africa.

Exploring Botswana and Namibia goes beyond just a one-time visit. Whether through books, conservation efforts, or staying engaged with fellow travelers, there are countless ways to deepen your understanding and appreciation for these incredible destinations.

Made in United States
Troutdale, OR
05/16/2025